South vs North

Compare two children – one born in north India, the other in the south.

The child from south India is far less likely to die in the first year of her life. She is less likely to lose her mother during childbirth and more likely to receive better nutrition.

She will also go to school and stay in school longer; she will more likely attend college. Compared to her peers in the north, she is less likely to be involved in agriculture, and the odds of her securing employment that pays her more are greater.

This child will also go on to have fewer children, who in turn will be healthier and more educated than her. In a nutshell, the average child born in south India will live a healthier, wealthier, more secure life than one born in north India.

Why is south India doing so much better than the north? And what does that mean?

In this superbly argued book, data scientist Nilakantan RS shows us not just how and why the southern states are outperforming the rest of the country but the consequence of the phenomenon in an India that is becoming increasingly centralized.

He reveals how south India deals with a particularly tough set of issues – its triumphs in areas of health, education and economic growth are met with a policy regime that penalizes it; its success in population control will be met with a possible loss of political representation. How will the region manage such an assault?

Hard-hitting, troubling and full of fascinating data points, *South vs North* is an essential book about one of the biggest challenges that India faces today.

South vs North

India's Great Divide

Nilakantan RS

JUGGERNAUT BOOKS
C-I-128, First Floor, Sangam Vihar, Near Holi Chowk,
New Delhi 110080, India

First published in hardback by Juggernaut Books 2022
Published in paperback by Juggernaut Books 2023

Copyright © Nilakantan RS 2022

10 9 8 7 6 5 4 3 2 1

P-ISBN: 9788195996933
E-ISBN: 9789393986399

The views and opinions expressed in this book are the author's own. The facts contained herein were reported to be true as on the date of publication by the author to the publishers of the book, and the publishers are not in any way liable for their accuracy or veracity.

All rights reserved. No part of this publication may be reproduced, transmitted, or stored in a retrieval system in any form or by any means without the written permission of the publisher.

Typeset in Adobe Caslon Pro by R. Ajith Kumar, Noida

Printed at Thomson Press India Ltd

*To Madras,
beloved and demanding home*

Contents

Introduction	1
Part I: Taking Stock	**13**
1. Health	15
2. Education	56
3. Economy	90
4. Why Has the South Performed Better?	128
Part II: India's Wicked Problems	**137**
Introduction: Is South India an Equal Partner?	139
1. Population Divergence	141
2. India's Purse Strings: Union vs States	165
3. Can the Indian Union be Salvaged in Its Current Form?	203
Part III: A More Perfect Union	**207**
Introduction: Imagining a Better Union	209
1. What Ails India's Representative Democracy?	213
2. The Athenian Model	234
3. An Alternative	246
Epilogue	263
Notes	267
A Note on the Author	270

Introduction

South India: A Different Country

Consider a child born in India.

This child is, firstly, far less likely to be born in south India than in north India, given the former's lower rates of population growth. But let's assume the child is born in the south. She is far less likely to die in the first year of her life given the lower infant mortality rates in south India compared to the rest of India. She is more likely to get vaccinated against diseases than the average Indian newborn, less likely to lose her mother during childbirth, more likely to get childcare services and receive better nutrition.

She is more likely to celebrate her fifth birthday, more likely to find a hospital or a doctor in case she falls sick, and more likely to eventually live a slightly longer life. She will also go to school and stay in school longer; she will more likely go to college than her contemporaries elsewhere in India. She is less likely to be involved in agriculture for economic sustenance and more likely to find work that pays her more.

She will also go on to be a mother to fewer children than her peers in the rest of India, and her children in turn will be healthier and more educated than she. And she'll have greater political representation and more impact on elections as a voter than those peers too. In short, the median child born in south India will live a healthier, wealthier, more secure and more socially impactful life than a child born in north India.

India's regional imbalance wasn't always skewed in favour of the south and it was never as substantial as it now is. At the time of Independence, the southern states were indistinguishable from the rest of India in terms of their development metrics. Today, the difference in development between some of the northern states and southern states is as stark as that between sub-Saharan Africa and the Organisation for Economic Co-operation and Development (OECD) countries.

Why is the south doing so much better than the north? Surely, it's not historical providence or ethnic essentialism, given their similar starting points. It's obviously not due to some policy implementation of the Government of India. That leaves policy decisions at the state level, the implementation capacity of their bureaucracies and dumb luck as other possible reasons. The capabilities of state bureaucracies are often realizations of policy decisions themselves. And luck, over a long enough period of time, is otherwise called policy vision and implementation.

So, why were states in southern India able to design better policy and implement it too? The literature credits subnationalism as one reason for the relatively better development of states in southern India.[1] In India, instances of subnationalism are often based on linguistic identity, given that they go back millennia. That sense of belonging in a localized geography is the glue which creates the knock-on effects that accelerate growth in various spheres, simply because we as a social species achieve great things when we have a common purpose.

Uttar Pradesh is often propped up as a counter-example to states with high levels of subnationalism. There's no subnationalism in that state. Even the name, Uttar Pradesh, is generic and was decided as an afterthought. It retains the colonial, short-version 'UP' for United Provinces and gives it a Hindustani twist. Unlike Tamil Nadu and Kerala, where linguistic identities transcended other subgroup identities, in Uttar Pradesh, loyalties to Hindi and Urdu served as proxies for religion. This continues to the present day in that state, where government programmes are often seen through the lens of caste groups or religious communities.

Compared to, say, Kerala, the trajectory of decay in public services in Uttar Pradesh, and its consequent status as a laggard state, runs in the opposite direction. The United Provinces under British rule was a relatively well-administered province while the princely state of Travancore, which is now part of Kerala, was a troubled place.

The economic trajectory of India's states follows the simple maxim of the modern era: the most important economic resource a country has is its people. A healthy and well-educated population with a reasonably well-run government is likely to have better economic prospects. The income levels and job prospects in south India, unsurprisingly, are significantly better than in the north.

Burden of Success

This success of the southern states, though, is under increasing pressure. The Indian Union, buoyed by the politics of nationalism, has sought to centralize policymaking. The declining significance of the southern states in national politics has coincided with the rise in prosperity in those regions. South India's concerns, to start with, are often orthogonal to those of north India, given the different stages of development they are in. South India also forms a demographically smaller section of the country.

The rise of nationalism as the dominant political ideology in northern India does not look at diversity in polity and policymaking as desirable. The demographic divergence between the north and south, which was already skewed in favour of the more populated north, has been made worse by a further skew in population growth that favours the north. All this makes south India a junior partner in the zero-sum game called electoral politics, diminishing its influence in decision-making.

The centralizing urge has been a feature of the Indian Union since its inception. In the twenty-first century, though, that complicated reality of India's democratic structure has assumed a cultural and political stranglehold over the country. Resource allocation by the Indian Union – whether of finances or other kinds of resources that the Union collects from and shares back with the states – heavily favours the north and works against the south. The south is taxed more, both in absolute terms and on a per capita basis, but receives far less allocation in return, simply because its population growth is lower.

The centralized collection and resource reallocation, especially of tax revenue, has meant states now have even less ability to either innovate in policy, or finance those innovations, than in the past. The Union, again because of how electoral politics works, has been designing policy for the northern and central plains of India and forcing that on the southern states. For example, a goal for the education sector, according to the National Education Policy (NEP) of 2020, is to reach 50 per cent enrolment in tertiary education by 2035. Some states in southern India have already exceeded that goal. Designing a policy whose fifteen-year goal has already been achieved is another way of condemning the south to status quo while waiting for the north to catch up.

There is a demographic detonation timed to go off in 2026, which will lead to another big fork in the future allocation of political power and associated resources between the north and south. Electoral delimitation – the periodic allocation and reallocation of seats on the basis of changes in population based on the census – was frozen in 1976, and that freeze is set to expire in 2026, when delimitation will be taken up again.

This process, which reapportions seats in Parliament based on population, decides how much of a say each state will have in the running of the country. South India is set to lose political representation – it already has a smaller representation in Parliament than the north – as a 'reward' for its effective population control. This comes exactly at a time when it needs more voices to highlight and fight the increased centralization in policymaking. This will effectively mean punishing policy success all over again.

The successes of south India have led to a really paradoxical situation: success in areas of health, education and economic growth is being met with a policy regime that penalizes it; success in population control will be met with a likely loss of political representation in 2026. How will the region cope with such an assault?

Tensions between India's constituent parts aren't new. This tussle began even as India came into being. The founder of the Dravida Munnetra Kazhagam (DMK), C.N. Annadurai, summed this up in his maiden speech in the Rajya Sabha over half a century ago. He raised questions that are central to the conception of India as a modern constitutional republic that was organized as a federal union. A frequently quoted section of his speech reads:

> I claim, Sir, to come from a country, a part in India now, but which I think is of a different stock, not necessarily antagonistic. I belong to the Dravidian stock. I am proud to call myself a Dravidian. That does not mean that I am

against a Bengali or a Maharashtrian or a Gujarati. As Robert Burns has stated, 'A man is a man for all that.' I say that I belong to the Dravidian stock and that is only because I consider that the Dravidians have got something concrete, something distinct, something different to offer to the nation at large. Therefore it is that we want self-determination.[2]

Annadurai did not state anything new and was only echoing what philosophers from the time of the ancient Greeks have been articulating in one form or another as accepted political rhetoric. Tragically, India's hyper-nationalist media environment of the twenty-first century reacts to transcripts of this speech, or rephrasings of it, as if it were treasonous. After all, the flourishing of the individual is a necessary condition for the flourishing of the collective, as the seventeeth-century Dutch philosopher Baruch Spinoza argued. The parts that constitute the union have to flourish if the union is to have any hope of flourishing.

India, however, has not been the most liberal in terms of its foundational nation-building. It did not ask territories that were part of the British Raj or the erstwhile princely states if they wanted to join the newly formed federal union through formal referendums. It did not use referendums to legitimize annexation of territories and populations, even in cases where this was an entirely plausible route.

The annexation of the territories that were ruled by the Nizam of Hyderabad, for example, provided an ideal case for asking the people of the territories whether they wanted to be part of the newly formed Indian Union or not. The population was largely in favour of such a move and had risen up against the Nizam. Yet no such question of seeking consent was considered.

Territorial ambitions at the time of its birth and territorial integrity ever since have been India's chief concern. The fears during and after Independence about the viability of the Union contributed to it, no doubt. The only referendum held was in Sylhet district in Assam in July 1947, and it opted for East Pakistan. This was before formal Independence.

After August 1947, the demand for independence, or autonomy, or some variant thereof, from various parts of independent India – from Nagaland to Kashmir to Punjab – have been met exclusively with force.

Most world leaders at the time of India's Independence thought the country would fail. And India seems to have acted in ways that sought to prove them wrong, whatever the costs. How will India, with its complicated structure of democracy and a difficult history, manage what promises to be a contentious and increasingly complex future?

India's Cleavages: Can They Be Managed?

The first part of this book will establish the divergence amongst Indian states in terms of their development metrics in health, education and economic prospects for their citizens. These core areas are considered over and above other metrics in other sectors, as they measure life at both the individual and demographic levels. They can also be measured objectively with relative ease. In addition, they are either the cause, or the effect, of every other measure in every other area.

Ranking states is a parlour game of sorts for politicians and the political press. The most recent anecdote or a cherry-picked statistic is often passed off as evidence in the process. Recently, the government itself started partaking in this 'game' with reports that were useful but had glaring errors in data and methodology that raised more questions than answers. The Good Governance Index, a yearly report that the Department of Administrative Reforms and Public Grievances puts out, for example, tracks year-on-year improvement in development metrics.

Some of the metrics that these government reports track are crucial and others not so critical; but they are all often equally weighted without sufficient discernment. The rationale for choosing the weights, wherever there are different weights, isn't clear either.

An example would be the state rankings for Commerce and Industry, where the scores are heavily influenced by the metrics of 'Ease of Doing Business' and 'Start-Up Ranking'. Both these metrics consider a wide range of input parameters that do not really reflect actual progress. This has resulted in absurd rankings, where Madhya Pradesh, a laggard state with little industry to speak of, was ranked ahead of India's most industrialized states in the 2019 report for Commerce and Industry.

Another, similar example concerns the NITI Aayog's tracking of Sustainable Development Goals (SDGs). NITI Aayog puts out an SDG India Index and Dashboard, which also falls into these familiar traps. The purpose of comparing states in these reports seems to be to rate the state governments of the day based on the policy prerogatives of the Union.

For instance, states are scored and ranked on their Aadhaar seeding and other centrally sponsored scheme implementations in the SDG India Index. It's a political report put out by a political executive. While there is a place for such reports, it's useful to take them with bagfuls of salt. The longer-term performance of states in real measures of development and well-being gets lost in such reports, particularly when the things that matter change too slowly for year-on-year improvement to be recorded.

As we compare the southern and northern states across parameters, we'll ask why the south has overtaken the north, and the ways in which the Centre is undercutting the south and what it means. These issues often manifest in the minutiae of budgeting, tax policy or allocation ratios. But their impact on actual lives is the most consequential.

In the second part, the book explores the effect of such divergence on the development metrics in an already diverse federal union. Given the peculiarities of India's political structure, it's especially negative, even devastating, in its impact on states in southern India. The ramifications get progressively worse too.

Many of these problems seem insurmountable. An easy, lazy and knee-jerk reaction is to seek or predict the balkanization of India, as Winston Churchill did. But many of the problems arise from poor transmission efficiency of the existing electoral structure.

The last section of the book re-examines the democratic structure of India and considers possible solutions to these problems. Can we re-imagine the democratic structure to improve transmission efficiency, avoid the threats of violence and balkanization and, therefore, find better ways to resolve the difficult resource allocation problems facing India?

One thought experiment is worth examining: A 'gamified' direct democracy that bridges the democracy of ancient Athens with modern guard rails to sidestep balkanization and yet achieve a decentralized polity. This would aim for enlightened liberalism achieved through conservative system design – something like a blockchain for democracy.

Part I

Taking Stock

1

Health

India's Health Report

It's axiomatic that the health of its individuals is a necessary condition for a society to thrive. For example, healthy individuals are, on average, materially more productive. The primary reason for a liberal society to provide healthcare to its citizens, though, is not to improve their economic output. It's a moral imperative, an end in itself. And that makes health outcomes a true measure of governance and social progress. This is especially relevant in developing countries, where lack of resources and poor literacy complicate an already difficult task.

Low- and middle-income societies have a vicious cycle on their hands. Their per capita income is not high, by definition. That means their ability to spend on healthcare is limited, resulting in poor health outcomes to start with. And poor health outcomes mean a diminished ability of the population to earn significantly to improve their economic situation, which in turn affects the society's future investments in healthcare. Developing countries, therefore, with very few exceptions, find it extremely difficult to break out of this trap.

India has a particularly poor health record. Its life expectancy at birth, the most basic measure of health of a population, is 69. That ranks it 125th in the world, behind war-torn countries like Iraq and Syria, and alongside Rwanda. Even in South Asia, a generally poor region of the world, India ranks behind its neighbours Sri Lanka, Bangladesh, Bhutan and Nepal in this respect. Only Pakistan has a lower life expectancy at birth.

India's infant mortality rate (IMR), a more robust and critical indicator, is also worse than most of its South Asian neighbours'. A major reason why life expectancy at birth in India is low is that, tragically, a lot of babies die soon after birth. Again, it's only Pakistan which does even worse than India in IMR in South Asia; our other neighbouring countries seem to let fewer infants die, despite most of them being poorer than us.

Diverging Stories

The story of India's performance in health, thus far, has been one of utter indifference to citizens' basic health. At the same time, our record is also one of extreme variance (see Table 1). Not all states are equally bad. Kerala, for instance, has an almost eleven-year advantage over Uttar Pradesh in terms of life expectancy at birth. That is, a child born in Kerala is expected to live an entire decade longer than a child born in Uttar Pradesh. The southern state, with a life expectancy at birth of 75, is comparable to upper-middle-income countries such as Argentina and Thailand. Uttar Pradesh, with life expectancy at birth of 64, has low-income countries such as Haiti, Liberia and Ethiopia as its peers.

Table 1: Life Expectancy at Birth, Census 2011

State	*Life Expectancy at Birth (Years)*
Andhra Pradesh	69
Assam	64
Bihar	68
Chhattisgarh	65
Gujarat	69
Haryana	69
Jharkhand	67
Karnataka	69
Kerala	75
Madhya Pradesh	64
Maharashtra	72
Odisha	66
Punjab	72
Rajasthan	68
Tamil Nadu	71
Uttar Pradesh	64
Uttarakhand	72
West Bengal	70

Source: Sample Registration System (SRS), Office of the Registrar General and Census Commissioner, Ministry of Home Affairs

The incidence of various diseases and their fatality rates are other commonly used indicators of the health of a population. These data measures are easily and readily available in developed countries, where they are published periodically, and, more importantly, are reliable.

In the developing world, however, health systems and hospitals do not publish disease-wise mortality reliably, which often leaves vital registrations – of births and deaths – as the only reliable source. While life expectancy at birth is one basic measure based on vital registrations, it does not capture the improvements in health systems robustly enough. By definition, this metric takes a lifetime to show up.

IMR is usually considered the strongest and most immediate measure of the health of a society in such cases. This is represented as the number of deaths per 1,000 live births.

Infants, naturally, need care when they are still infants. And when infants die, tragic as that is, it becomes a good metric to track since there is no time lag in the data showing up in the IMR, unlike deaths among the overall population. Infants also form one of the most vulnerable sections of the population.

The question of health and survival of infants is a great leveller in terms of care-seeking behaviours of a population too. It thus serves as a good test of the efficacy of a healthcare system. The factors that prevent infant mortality, to a large extent, happen to be basic healthcare practices that do not need high-end facilities; this makes it a less unequal playing field. More importantly, the statistics around the IMR are easy to collect, even in poor countries with skeletal bureaucracies; it is a mere count of births and deaths, just as with life expectancy, but on a compressed time scale. The IMR, therefore, is robust, easy to measure and difficult to fudge.

India, as a whole, had an IMR of 32 in 2018, according to the Sample Registration System (SRS) Bulletin – that is, 32 deaths per 1,000 live births. This ranks India alongside Kenya (31), Eritrea (31) and Senegal (32); significantly worse than war-torn Syria (14) and Iraq (23). But to use one metric for all of India would be misleading (see Table 2).

Table 2: IMR in India by State, May 2020

State	*IMR*
Andhra Pradesh	29
Assam	41
Bihar	32
Chhattisgarh	41
Gujarat	28
Haryana	30
Jharkhand	30
Karnataka	23
Kerala	7
Madhya Pradesh	48
Maharashtra	19
Odisha	40
Punjab	20

State	IMR
Rajasthan	37
Tamil Nadu	15
Telangana	27
Uttar Pradesh	43
Uttarakhand	31
West Bengal	22

Note: IMR is number of deaths per 1000 live births
Source: Sample Registration System (SRS)-Bulletin 2020, Vol. 55, No. 1, Office of the Registrar General and Census Commissioner, Ministry of Home Affairs, May 2020

Kerala, India's best-performing state on health parameters, had an IMR of 7 in 2018; for comparison, the United States, the world's most powerful country, had an IMR of 6. Tamil Nadu, the state next door to Kerala and India's second-best state on health parameters, had an IMR of 15. That puts the state in the league of upper-middle-income countries. States such as Maharashtra (19), Punjab (20), West Bengal (22) and Karnataka (23) manage to sneak in ahead of, or are on par with, war-ravaged Iraq.

Madhya Pradesh, meanwhile, was India's worst state by this metric, with an IMR of 48. Not only does Madhya Pradesh rank last, it's also the only state where the IMR got worse with time – from 47 in 2016 to 48 in 2018. Niger and Afghanistan, both war-torn, violence-ridden and deeply unstable countries, also had an IMR of 48 in 2018.

This wide-ranging IMR – from 7 to 48 – straddling the gulf between the United States and Afghanistan – among large states with populations larger than most European countries, is what makes the use of a single metric for all of India hopelessly inadequate to portray the reality. Describing India with one metric is as accurate as describing the planet with one metric.

An interesting quirk with regard to the data on IMR is the divergence between SRS and National Family Health Survey (NFHS-4) data. Kerala, as seen above, had an IMR of 7 for 2018 according to the SRS Bulletin; Kerala's IMR was 6, according to NFHS-4 for 2016. Uttar Pradesh had an IMR of 43, according to the SRS, and 64 according to NFHS-4. That is, the discrepancy between the two data sources doesn't go just one way for all states. Instead, it may enlarge the divergence between the best and worst states, particularly at the bottom end.

However, if one thinks about the methodologies used by the two surveys, the reason for their divergence becomes apparent. The SRS indicates, is an actual count and depends on registrations of births and deaths. The NFHS is a demographic survey. It asks people in a survey about children and infants who may have died.

In states where the ratios of registrations of births to actual births and the rate of institutional births (that is, within medical facilities) are low, it is likely that the SRS may undercount infant deaths. After all, it is difficult to count an infant death from a registry if the birth of that infant was never registered in the first place. So, the real IMR for states at the bottom of the pile may be even worse than the SRS data reveals.

The IMR as a metric, despite these quirks, has been so robust that it has been found to predict general health outcomes of the society at large. It is easy to understand why: improving the IMR means improving basic care, which by definition results in better overall health outcomes for the entire population. Some studies suggest a high IMR is even correlated with political instability and violent revolutions. Again, one can intuitively grasp why that would be the case – a society that abandons basic health is a deeply troubled one.

Another metric related to the IMR is the Under Five Mortality Rate (U5MR) which measures deaths of children under the age of five for every 1,000 live births (IMR measures deaths of infants under the age of one). The U5MR, like the IMR, is a metric that serves not just as a measure of the health of children but of society at large. And in India, just like infants, children under five die at a higher rate than in all its neighbouring countries except Pakistan.

Again, the variance among the large states is wide-ranging. Kerala at 9 and Tamil Nadu at 17 have the lowest rates among states, according to the SRS for the year 2015, while Uttar Pradesh at 44 is India's worst state on this parameter. Maharashtra, a state that's peninsular but not quite southern, is another consistently good performer on the IMR and U5MR.

A particularly troubling aspect of child mortality in India is that girl children die at higher rates than boys. This exacerbates an already dismal situation, where fewer girls are born in the first place due to sex-selective abortions. The divergence between India's best and worst states is even

Table 3: IMR and U5MR by State, 2015–16

State	IMR	U5MR
Kerala	6	7
Tamil Nadu	20	27
Maharashtra	24	29
Karnataka	27	31
Punjab	29	33
West Bengal	28	32
Jammu and Kashmir	32	38
Haryana	33	41
Gujarat	34	43
Himachal Pradesh	34	38
Andhra Pradesh	35	41
Telangana	28	32
Odisha	40	48
Rajasthan	41	51
Jharkhand	44	54
Assam	48	56
Bihar	48	58
Madhya Pradesh	51	65
Chhattisgarh	54	64
Uttar Pradesh	64	78

Note: IMR and U5MR are calculated on the basis of number of deaths per 1000 live births
Source: National Family Health Survey (NFHS-4), 2015–16: India, International Institute for Population Sciences, 2017

wider for U5MR than it is for the IMR when we consider NFHS-4 data. Again, since there are more children under five than there are under one, and given the methodological differences, this is not unexpected.

Table 4: U5MR, 2015

State	U5MR
Andhra Pradesh*	29
Assam	34
Bihar	37
Chhattisgarh	38
Gujarat	28
Haryana	34
Jharkhand	27
Karnataka	28
Kerala	9
Madhya Pradesh	40
Maharashtra	18
Odisha	39
Punjab	24
Rajasthan	32
Tamil Nadu	17
Telangana*	NA
Uttar Pradesh	44
West Bengal	26

Note: U5MR is number of deaths per 1000 live births
* Data for Andhra Pradesh and Telangana have not been disaggregated
Source: NITI Aayog

A third metric that is related to childbirth is maternal mortality ratio (MMR). This is calculated as the number of maternal deaths per 100,000 live births. It reveals the responsiveness of a healthcare system to women in particular.

One of the biggest advancements in healthcare all across the world in the twentieth century was the improvement in the MMR.

Table 5: MMR, 2015–17

State	MMR
Assam	229
Bihar	165
Jharkhand	76
Madhya Pradesh	188
Chhattisgarh	141
Odisha	168
Rajasthan	186
Uttar Pradesh	216
Andhra Pradesh	74
Telangana	76
Karnataka	97
Kerala	42
Tamil Nadu	63
Gujarat	87
Haryana	98
Maharashtra	55
Punjab	122
West Bengal	94

Note: MMR is number of deaths per 1000 live births
Source: Special Bulletin on Maternal Mortality in India 2015–17, Office of the Registrar General and Census Commissioner, Ministry of Home Affairs, March 2022

Sadly, though, India ranked 130th among the world's nations in this metric in 2017, behind Pakistan and just ahead of Bolivia. Within India, as with the other two childbirth-related metrics, there is wide variance. A woman who is giving birth in Uttar Pradesh is four times more likely to die during childbirth than a woman giving birth in Kerala. Peninsular India, in general, again does far better than the rest of India on this count.

Tackling high IMR, U5MR and MMR takes real governance and hard work. The strategies to reduce mortalities related to childbirth are straightforward, but they call for time, effort, long-term commitment and budgetary support from state governments. For example, one metric that IMR, UFMR and MMR are all inversely correlated to is the percentage of institutional deliveries. The higher the number of institutional deliveries, the lower the IMR, MMR and UFMR (see Chart 1).

High mortality among infants, children and mothers during childbirth is easily preventable with the most basic of care. But for this to happen, basic care must be made available widely. Functional hospitals and primary health centres (PHCs) are obviously a necessary condition for high rates of institutional deliveries and low mortality rates during childbirth. Unsurprisingly, the five southern states rank as the five best states in terms of institutional delivery, and the rates of institutional deliveries drop significantly as one travels north (see Table 6).

Health

Chart 1: IMR vs Institutional Deliveries

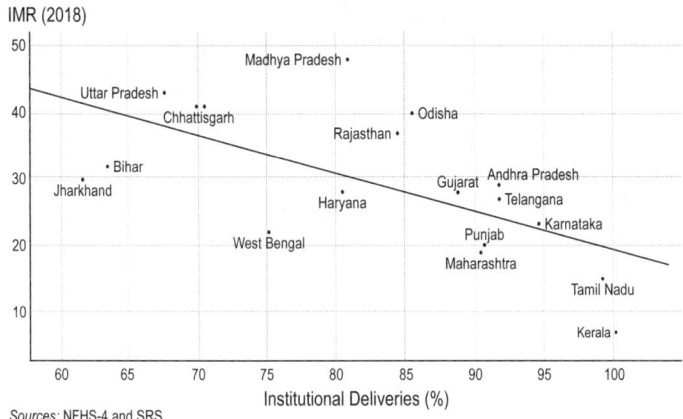

Sources: NFHS-4 and SRS

Table 6: Institutional Deliveries

State/UT	Total (As % of All Births)
Andhra Pradesh	92
Assam*	71
Bihar*	64
Chhattisgarh*	70
Gujarat	89
Haryana	81
Jharkhand*	62
Karnataka	94
Kerala	100
Madhya Pradesh*	81
Maharashtra	90
Odisha*	85
Punjab	91

State/UT	Total (As % of All Births)
Rajasthan*	84
Tamil Nadu	99
Telangana	92
Uttar Pradesh*	68
West Bengal	75

* States where Annual Health Survey (AHS) data was used.
Sources: NFHS-4 and Annual Health Survey (AHS), Vital Statistics Division Office, Registrar General and Census Commissioner

Health Infrastructure Across States

The rates of survival of infants, children, young mothers and the entire population are divergent in the extreme among India's states. The likely reason for such divergences is the underlying differences in infrastructure.

Health infrastructure in rural India largely means the presence of well-functioning PHCs in remote villages. These PHCs need to have the ability to provide maternity services. This includes having functional operation theatres, having a doctor who shows up regularly for duty, having nurses/staff who are well trained, and having medicines readily available. Another crucial piece of infrastructure, which many of the southern states have, is a well-functioning emergency ambulance network that ferries complicated cases to the nearest tertiary care hospital when the PHCs are not able to deal with an emergency, or are not equipped to.

This requires thoughtful planning and committed implementation, which do not always fetch immediate results. Incentive programmes for doctors to serve in these remote villages and reward programmes for health workers to stay motivated have all been important factors in successful states. By their very nature, such long-term policies yield results in time frames that outlast the electoral cycle. State governments thus have to work for what is beyond their narrow self-interest.

That enduring truth of medicine – that prevention is better than cure – applies to childbirth and related mortality too. So, even more important than critical care at the time of childbirth is antenatal care and support for pregnant women. It has a greater impact on controlling the IMR, U5MR, and MMR than anything done after the mother or child develop complications.

This, however, involves healthcare workers walking the streets of villages and administering care to anyone who is, or is likely to be, pregnant. It is a difficult and complex administrative task that does not get the headlines. It comes to fruition slowly, bringing little reward in the next election.

Another crucial contributor towards better child health is better nutrition. Well-fed children are less likely to die when young; they also grow up to become healthier and materially more productive adults compared with malnourished children. A child's ability to stay in school too dramatically improves with nutrition. India's children, though, have been plagued by poor nutrition. Uttar Pradesh, Bihar and Jharkhand have almost half their children under five years of age showing stunted growth; these very states, predictably, have high child mortality. South India, again, has a much lower ratio of children with stunted growth.

Table 7: Children Under 5 Years Who Are Stunted

State	Stunted Children (%)
Kerala	20
Punjab	26
Tamil Nadu	27
Andhra Pradesh	31
West Bengal	33
Haryana	34
Odisha	34
Maharashtra	34
Karnataka	36
Assam	36
Chhattisgarh	38
Gujarat	39
Rajasthan	39
Madhya Pradesh	42
Jharkhand	45
Uttar Pradesh	46
Bihar	48

Source: National Family Health Survey (NFHS-4), 2015–16: India, International Institute for Population Sciences, 2017

India now deals with child nutrition and child health, particularly in the case of poor children in the rural areas, through the Integrated Child Development Services

(ICDS) Scheme. This umbrella programme funds several initiatives, including childcare shelters, or Anganwadis, for early childhood programmes and interventions.

Anganwadi centres have grown from being informal set-ups to becoming state-funded formal early childhood programmes. In the last few decades, they have been rolled into central programmes – that is, programmes implemented by the states and funded largely by the Union. They provide daycare, supplemental nutrition, health checks, immunization, and other aspects of basic care for children and parents working in otherwise trying circumstances and living in extreme poverty.

The first and obvious test of a state's responsivity to newborn children is how many of those births are registered and how many of the newborns issued birth certificates. After all, a state will not be able to plan or execute any programme unless it knows how many children are born, and where.

In Rajasthan, Bihar, Uttar Pradesh and Jharkhand, less than a third of all births in 2014 were registered within twenty-one days. In Tamil Nadu, Kerala and Gujarat, by contrast, more than 90 per cent of all new births were registered within twenty-one days (see Table 8). This, again, is understandable, since institutional births have a high correlation with registration of births.

Table 8: Children Aged 0–4 Whose Births Are Registered Within 21 Days of Birth

State	Children (%)
Delhi	80
Haryana	81
Himachal Pradesh	78
Punjab	81
Uttar Pradesh	27
Uttarakhand	58
Chhattisgarh	40
Madhya Pradesh	67
Bihar	32
Jharkhand	25
Odisha	38
West Bengal	85
Assam	78
Rajasthan	33
Goa	97
Gujarat	91
Maharashtra	80
Andhra Pradesh	56
Karnataka	84
Kerala	92

Source: Rapid Survey on Children (RSOC), 2013–14, Ministry of Women and Child Development

The basic metrics of Anganwadi centres can tell us how well they function. They need a proper building, for example, to shelter children and inspire confidence among the parents.

Those buildings must have toilets. Each centre would need a separate kitchen to cook and serve meals to children in need of nutritious food. There must be as few disruptions as possible in the functioning of these centres. They need equipment like weighing machines to monitor the health and nutrition status of the children they serve. In each of these metrics, the familiar pattern of southern states running these ICDS programmes well and fetching good outcomes, emerges (see Tables 9, 10, 11 and 12).

Table 9: Anganwadis in 'Pucca' Building

State	*Anganwadis (%)*
Andhra Pradesh	64
Assam	92
Bihar	67
Haryana	100
Jharkhand	75
Karnataka	60
Kerala	98
Madhya Pradesh	85
Maharashtra	84
Rajasthan	97
Tamil Nadu	100
Telangana	80
Uttar Pradesh	93
West Bengal	9

Source: Visit to Anganwadi Centres – State Specific Report, 2017–18, Central Monitoring Unit, Monitoring and Evaluation Division National Institute of Public Cooperation and Child Development

Table 10: Usable Toilets in Anganwadis

State	Usable Toilets (%)
Andhra Pradesh	72
Assam	27
Bihar	13
Haryana	86
Jharkhand	18
Karnataka	100
Kerala	92
Madhya Pradesh	45
Maharashtra	68
Rajasthan	57
Tamil Nadu	73
Telangana	70
Uttar Pradesh	33
West Bengal	29

Source: Visit to Anganwadi Centres – State Specific Report 2017–18, Central Monitoring Unit, Monitoring and Evaluation Division National Institute of Public Cooperation and Child Development

Table 11: Availability of Baby Weighing Machines in Anganwadis

State	Baby Weighing Machines (%)
Andhra Pradesh	100
Assam	19
Bihar	67
Haryana	100

State	Baby Weighing Machines (%)
Jharkhand	38
Karnataka	100
Kerala	100
Madhya Pradesh	70
Maharashtra	74
Rajasthan	58
Tamil Nadu	100
Telangana	80
Uttar Pradesh	20
West Bengal	88

Source: Visit to Anganwadi Centres – State Specific Report 2017–18, Central Monitoring Unit, Monitoring and Evaluation Division National Institute of Public Cooperation and Child Development

Table 12: Anganwadis with Separate Kitchens

State	Separate Kitchens (%)
Andhra Pradesh	84
Assam	59
Bihar	10
Haryana	77
Jharkhand	55
Karnataka	100
Kerala	100
Madhya Pradesh	35
Maharashtra	71
Rajasthan	36
Tamil Nadu	100

State	Separate Kitchens (%)
Telangana	100
Uttar Pradesh	23
West Bengal	6

Source: Visit to Anganwadi Centres – State Specific Report 2017–18, Central Monitoring Unit, Monitoring and Evaluation Division National Institute of Public Cooperation and Child Development

The health of infants and young children and their mothers, it appears, is not only a measure of the health of a society but also of its overall resolve towards improving the lives of its citizens. That societies with better resolve do a better job of providing healthcare is tautological.

Societies with similar starting points and economic status but divergent outcomes over a generation, though, provide an example of where that resolve explains the divergence. Running a well-functioning state-wide ICDS programme, just like running a PHC network, requires considerable work and attention to detail. The work will appear thankless in the short term. Citizens' seeing these services as necessary and voting in incumbents for trying out the right things, therefore, becomes a crucial intangible condition for delivering better health in the longer term.

A crucial aspect of health systems, as with all other systems, is the equilibrium between demand and supply. In healthcare, what makes up demand is – above all – the number of people in the community and the rate at which the population is growing. The total fertility rate (TFR) of a state, which tells us how many children are born to each woman, informs us of each state's health in an indirect but most important way.

One of the most pressing problems in India in most matters is that there are too few resources to meet the needs of too many people. A low fertility rate means there are fewer births in the first place so that the state's infrastructure isn't strained to meet the demand. Secondly, a low fertility rate also means access to contraception, higher literacy among women and higher awareness among the population: all of which are signs of a healthy society. Women who have fewer children are also able to attend to their children better and offer better care through the first five years of the child's life, when the child is most vulnerable. South India produces fewer babies and takes better care of them without stretching the limits of its delivery system.

In the chart plotting TFR versus IMR (Chart 2), southern Indian states seem to have achieved better health outcomes by investing in better health infrastructure. It's been a feature of their politics as well, which has fed into a virtuous cycle of successive governments wanting to be seen as doing something towards better health outcomes for their people.

A 'side effect' of a literate state that has a strong care-seeking behaviour is that the greater demand for care drives up the price of healthcare. This has meant that Kerala, the state that has the highest literacy and best metrics in terms of basic health outcomes, is also the most expensive state for medical treatment.

Chart 2: TFR vs IMR

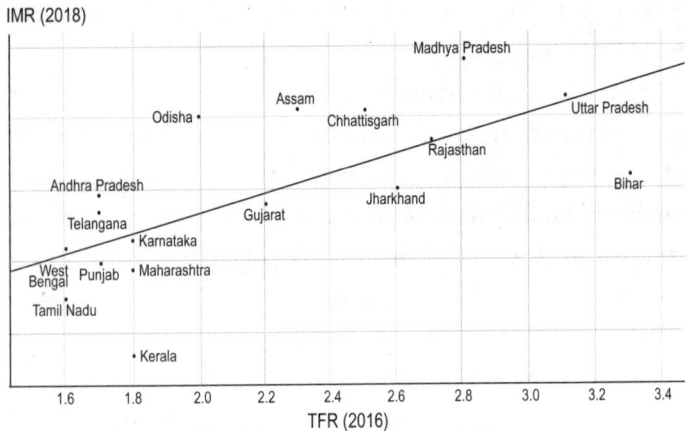

Sources: *Sample Registration System (SRS)-Statistical Report 2016*, Office of the Registrar General and Census Commissioner, 2017 and *Sample Registration System (SRS), Bulletin* 2020, Vol. 55, No. 1, Office of the Registrar General and Census Commissioner, May 2020

South India: Why Is It Healthier?

The Government of India started releasing an annual Good Governance Index at the end of 2019. This measured various states across various sectors, with metrics for each of those sectors. Some of these sectors and the methods used for the metrics were controversial. In the case of some others, such as health, the metrics were straightforward and universally accepted. The health sector, for instance, was measured on the basis of IMR, MMR, TFR, immunization performance, availability of doctors at PHCs, and operationalization of 24x7 facilities at PHCs. Measured thus, the top two states, predictably, were Kerala and Tamil Nadu in 2019 (see Tables 13 and 14).

Table 13: Number of Beds in Public Hospitals

State	No. of Public Hospital Beds (Per Million of Population)
Andhra Pradesh	438
Assam	496
Bihar	98
Chhattisgarh	329
Gujarat	316
Haryana	410
Jharkhand	289
Karnataka	1,054
Kerala	1,076
Madhya Pradesh	378
Maharashtra	426
Odisha	408
Punjab	606
Rajasthan	601
Tamil Nadu	1,014
Telangana	545
Uttar Pradesh	333
West Bengal	804

Source: Data as uploaded by states on the Health Management Information System (HMIS) portal. Status as on 20 July 2018.

Table 14: Mothers Who Had at Least 4 Antenatal Care Visits, 2015–16

State	4 or More Antenatal Care Visits (%)
Andhra Pradesh	76
Assam	46
Bihar	14
Chhattisgarh	59
Gujarat	71
Haryana	45
Jharkhand	30
Karnataka	70
Kerala	90
Madhya Pradesh	36
Maharashtra	72
Odisha	62
Punjab	68
Rajasthan	39
Tamil Nadu	81
Telangana	75
Uttar Pradesh	26
West Bengal	76

Source: National Family Health Survey (NFHS-4), 2015–16: India, International Institute for Population Sciences, 2017

Southern Indian states, as the data so far has revealed, have better health outcomes and better infrastructure to deliver basic health-related services. That better health services result in better health outcomes is obvious. But why do the southern states have better services that have resulted in better outcomes?

Table 15: Improvement in IMR, 1981 vs 2018

State	1981	2018	Improvement (%)
Madhya Pradesh	142	48	66
Assam	106	41	61
Odisha	135	40	70
Uttar Pradesh	150	43	71
Rajasthan	108	37	66
Bihar	118	32	73
Andhra Pradesh	86	29	66
Haryana	101	28	72
Gujarat	116	28	76
West Bengal	91	22	76
Karnataka	69	23	67
Punjab	81	20	75
Maharashtra	79	19	76
Tamil Nadu	91	15	84
Kerala	37	7	81

Source: SRS Bulletin, Office of the Registrar General and Census Commissioner, Ministry of Home Affairs

Take the case of Tamil Nadu, the state with the best record in improving its IMR (see Table 15). This is also the state that innovated the most in antenatal care and invested the most in PHCs. The state, beginning in the early

1990s, started rewarding healthcare workers who achieved zero IMR in the areas they were responsible for with gold coins. The PHC which achieved the greatest decline in IMR in the state earned both its medical officer and the district to which it belonged, rolling shields. Village health nurses were incentivized with cash rewards when women chose institutional deliveries over home deliveries. Pregnant women themselves were given significant cash incentives to get their babies delivered at PHCs.

The state government established the Tamil Nadu Medical Services Corporation with the primary objective of ensuring ready availability of all essential drugs and medicines at public health facilities by adopting a streamlined procedure for their procurement, storage and distribution. The result of all of these initiatives has been a steady drop in IMR.

It is important to note in this context that states that are currently doing well on IMR/U5MR were not always states at the top of the ranking table. For example, Tamil Nadu's IMR in 1971 (Table 15 is from 1981, by which time it had improved to 91) was 113. The state ranked lower than Maharashtra (105), Punjab (102), Karnataka (95) and Andhra Pradesh (106). In 2018, Tamil Nadu had a lower IMR than all those states and every other state in India except Kerala.

In terms of rate of improvement, Tamil Nadu did even better than Kerala and was the state with the steepest fall in infant and child mortality. It is not mere happenstance that states with good services in basic care and early childhood health have achieved low rates of child mortality.

Maharashtra has been a consistently good performer in terms of saving its youngest. Karnataka and Andhra Pradesh have improved in providing basic health services, which put them in the broad 'southern bucket'. There are pick-up and drop services for pregnant women in Karnataka and a robust ambulance network in Andhra Pradesh, for example, which have contributed greatly to their improved numbers.

Peninsular India, in general, has low child mortality because the state governments addressed each contributing factor to high child mortality using a government service. Some of them worked; many did not. Many of them probably had leaks in the system – which is known to the public as corruption. But the slow march towards better outcomes was a constant in these southern states that had resolved to improve their health status.

Rich States vs Poor States

Does good health follow a good economic situation, or does it result in one? This is a question that researchers have grappled with for a long time. The evidence has been complicated and the answer is not very clear. The Indian experience, as one would expect, is mixed as well. Rich states have not always performed as well as we would expect them to; sometimes their performance has been an utter disappointment.

For example, Haryana, a relatively prosperous state, records an IMR that is far worse than that of several states that are less wealthy. Within the Indian context, some states, such as Kerala and West Bengal, do better than their economic status predicts, as the graph plotting IMR versus state per capita income shows (Chart 3).

Chart 3: IMR vs Per Capita Net State Domestic Product (NSDP)

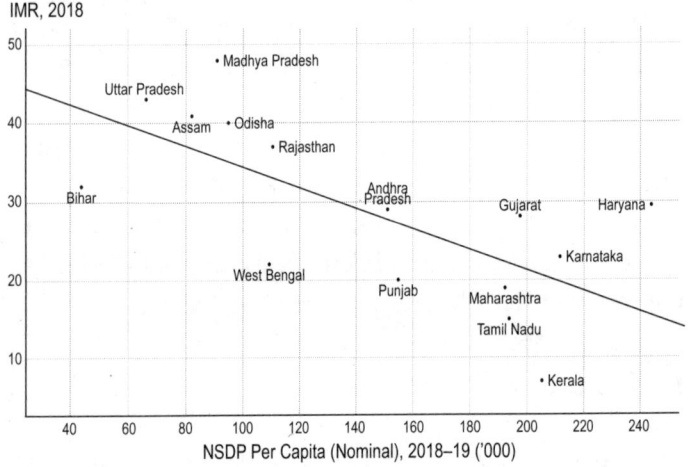

Sources: SRS Bulletins, May 2019 and Ministry of Statistics and Programme Implementation (MOSPI)

If there was a complete inverse correlation between income and health, we would get a straight trend line when plotting IMR versus per capita; as per capita rises, the IMR should drop.

A given state's resolve to deliver effective healthcare can be measured by looking at the variation from such a straight trend line (the residual from the overall trend line, as it is known) when we plot IMR against per capita income. Haryana stands out in showing a clear absence of such resolve and its callousness towards its children, since its IMR is far higher than expected; while West Bengal, despite being relatively poor, does a decent job, since its IMR is lower than expected.

In general, however, it does seem true that richer states do better. Similarly, other factors such as institutional birth, hospital beds per million, etc., also seem to have an effect, as one would expect, on IMR and U5MR. More hospital beds also seem to result in lower IMR, for example (see Chart 4).

Chart 4: IMR vs Number of Beds in Government Hospitals

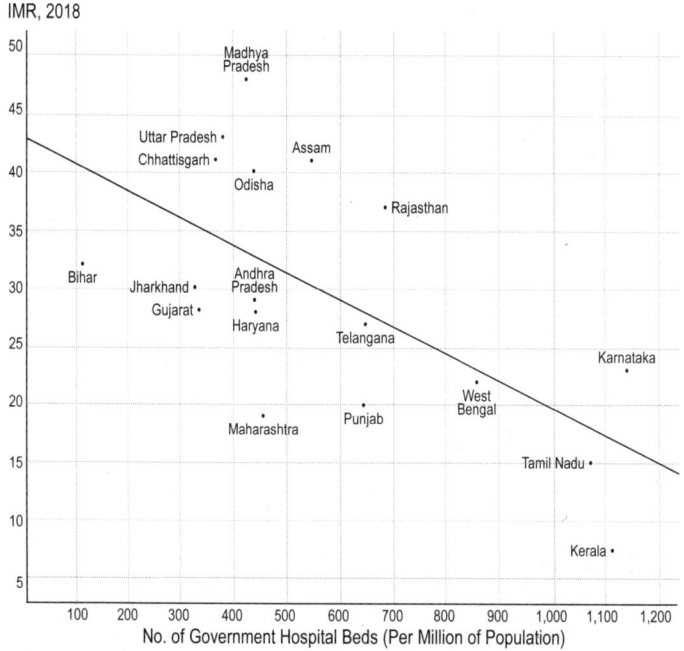

Sources: HMIS and SRS

In other words, having resources is a basic requirement for health, but the resolve to prioritize health matters too.

Beyond the mortality factors related to childbirth and the nutritional support systems for children, the overall capacity of each state, in terms of total doctors and beds available in government facilities measured per capita, tells us how a society is prepared to face a health crisis.

These are conventional metrics which cater to the health of the overall population – as is the number of doctors that each state produces each year. Southern India in general leads on these health infrastructure measures when compared with other large states. Karnataka, despite being roughly a fourth of Uttar Pradesh in population size, produces way more doctors (see Table 16).

Table 16: Number of Registered Doctors

State	*No. of Registered Doctors (Per Million of Population)*
Andhra Pradesh	1,098
Assam	337
Bihar	637
Chhattisgarh	125
Gujarat	755
Haryana	71
Jharkhand	93
Karnataka	1,275
Kerala	594

State	No. of Registered Doctors (Per Million of Population)
Madhya Pradesh	473
Maharashtra	1,920
Odisha	264
Punjab	534
Rajasthan	517
Tamil Nadu	1,353
Telangana	54
Uttar Pradesh	1,144
West Bengal	958

Note: Telangana counts only New Registration after the state formation
Source: Medical Council of India (MCI)

Whichever way one looks at the data – whether on the basis of the latest absolute values of child mortality, or the historical status of the various states, or their trajectory of progress over the years, or in terms of the relative performance of each state in terms of per capita income or establishment of health infrastructure – southern and peninsular India do better than the central and northern parts of the country.

One Nation, One Doctor

Given the performance of the southern states, particularly Kerala and Tamil Nadu, one would assume that the rest of India would emulate them, with other states trying to copy their successful programmes and tailor them to their own unique circumstances. But in India, the Union government seems to be doing the opposite: it is trying to centralize India's healthcare and then force the more successful states to follow the centralized approach.

Running one-size-fits-all programmes from Delhi has always been a suboptimal way of functioning. Yet, the Union government runs multiple centrally sponsored schemes and flagship programmes in the area of health. There are now centrally sponsored health insurance programmes and cash incentives for institutional deliveries. These were both successful state-run programmes in much of southern India before they became watered-down central programmes. The Union government's argument that it is copying good programmes at the state level is naive at best and often just an excuse for erosion of states' rights.

The various stages of development of the different states in India demand varying programmes with differing emphasis on which parameters to focus on. A single programme for incentivizing institutional delivery across all states, for example, does not even pause to ascertain whether a wide network of PHCs exists in all those states, and whether these are well staffed.

Similarly, the various schemes relating to midday meals, childcare and early intervention have been rolled out under the ICDS programme into a fully centralized concept. These central health programmes increase the reporting burden for the state bureaucracies and often end up being programmes conceived in New Delhi that aren't tailored to local needs and don't have buy-in from the states.

The central flagship health programme, the National Health Mission encompasses two sub-missions: the National Rural Health Mission and the National Urban Health Mission. Most of the goals of these missions have already been achieved by some of the southern states. Let us take the example of the top four goals, which are:
- Reduction of MMR to 1/1,000 live births
- Reduction of IMR to 25/1,000 live births
- Reduction of TFR to 2.1
- Prevention and reduction of anaemia in women aged 15–49 years

Kerala has had an IMR of less than 25/1,000 for a couple of generations now, while Tamil Nadu achieved it a generation ago. As has Maharashtra. Karnataka, too, achieved this goal recently. These states also have MMRs and TFRs that are well below the recommended targets.

A national programme thus defeats the purpose of goal-setting for the more advanced states. What is worse is that it does this while explicitly taking the power of policymaking away from the states. It is one thing to set up broad goals that do not have a real impact on a state, and entirely another to tie these goals to funding that helps achieve those goals. The National Health Mission has been hurtling towards the latter at an alarming rate. Its programmes, such as incentivization of institutional delivery, are problematic at the national level for this reason.

The combined expenditure in the Union budget for the

centrally sponsored schemes of the National Health Mission, ICDS umbrella programmes and the Midday Meal Scheme was Rs 62,658 crore in 2018–19. For 2020–21, the budget estimate was Rs 73,672 crore.

That is a significant chunk of money, their share of which states will not want to forgo. Yet that is money for plans and programmes of declining priority for the southern states, given their progress thus far. It is not that there is a different programme or policy that the Union government can run, which would magically be more just to all states. The vast divergence between the states makes any single programme for every one of them a logical impossibility, however well-meaning it may be.

It is also in this context that the decision by the Union government to implement the National Eligibility Cum Entrance Test (NEET) comes as a body blow to state-level progress made in health. Medical schools produce the most important resource in running a healthcare system: doctors. The ability to tweak the parameters so that most of the doctors produced in a state stay back in the state to provide healthcare to the most vulnerable sections of that state is a necessary tool for any state to have if it is going to provide healthcare to its citizens. What NEET does is take this tool away from the state's toolkit.

Karnataka, for example, produces the most number of doctors for any state in the country. Maharashtra has the highest number of doctors as a ratio of its population, followed by Tamil Nadu and Kerala. Andhra Pradesh follows its neighbours in southern India, producing a relatively large number of doctors given its population and having a large number of hospital beds in tertiary care facilities.

These states, each with their own quirks, were running their own medical education systems. The state governments in the southern states have tried to deploy the relatively large number of doctors they produce in the rural areas to provide health services at their PHCs. Tamil Nadu, for example, had a system of incentivizing doctors who served in its PHCs by offering them preferential admission for advanced studies. For this reason, Tamil Nadu also has one of the highest ratios among all states in terms of the number of doctors at its PHCs to the population. Karnataka imposed mandatory rural service for students upon their graduation from medical school.

In Tamil Nadu's case, the state had an affirmative action/reservation policy that was different from the rest of India; it had a higher ratio of seats reserved for historically disadvantaged communities, which has resulted in doctors who are more representative of the population. Doctors being demographically diverse and being reflective of the population has proved to be a significant factor in improving care the world over. After all, in a caste-ridden society, it is likely that the doctor–patient relationship will also fall victim to such prejudice. A skewed demographic of doctors who aren't representative of the population they are treating is only likely to increase the barriers that block those from oppressed communities from seeking healthcare.

NEET removes the power of states to run their medical education programmes as they deem fit. And it's these innovations at the state level in producing healthcare's most important resource – doctors – that have resulted in overall improvements in population-level health metrics for the better performing states.

The southern states will have a very different set of challenges in the next decade or two from the rest of India. Their populations are older, owing to their having had below-replacement TFR for a generation. The southern states have the highest ratio of people over sixty years of age in their population. While states like Kerala and Tamil Nadu have achieved great results in reducing child mortality, the challenge ahead is geriatric care, as the experience of countries and societies with ageing populations has shown. That means the focus on healthcare expenditure has to be very different for these states from that for the rest of India, where TFR is still above replacement levels or has only just come under.

Southern India, for example, has seen an increasing trend of obesity and diabetes in its population. The solution to that, which is to reduce caloric intake and improve the nutritional composition of the diet, is at odds with much of what northern and central India are trying to solve – namely, insufficient caloric intake.

Similarly, given the high-base effect, the improvements in IMR/U5MR/MMR for northern India are likely to be much higher than for southern India. Thus, incentivizing improvements with a uniform structure would be an impossible task. Above all, these two societies, as their politics have shown, value health outcomes differently. What does a democracy and a federal union do in such a situation?

It is natural for populations in states that are not doing well in terms of health outcomes to wish for better outcomes. Politicians, naturally, will promise the electorate what they seek in a democracy. However, the problem is that when the promise is made at the wrong level of government in a federal union like India, it ends up creating a power imbalance. This imbalance inevitably skews the structure in favour of the Union, given the Union government owns most of the sources of revenue.

It is somewhat obvious, therefore, that most of the new health programmes that are run by the Union government fall in the category of extension of monetary help to citizens. These are administered either through specific funds, or through insurance or other similar assistance – without seeking inputs from state governments on what they would do with that money if they had a say in it.

Having a centralized programme – which is largely a cash giveaway programme for health according to parameters set in Delhi – as opposed to having state-level programmes run by the respective states, serves no real purpose except in moving political credit to the Centre. After all, the Union government does not control hospitals or doctors or PHCs or any other medical infrastructure on the ground. At least not yet, though it seems to be seeking exactly that through initiatives like NEET.

Conversely, India's research capacity in health, which would be a legitimate central function in a federal union, is still woefully inadequate. Research, much like the running of antenatal programmes, has a long gestation period. Governments may change before research projects come to fruition. And the Union government – successive ones at that – have focused on gaining political credit for cash transfers and have not achieved long-term results from that. This only tells us that at least some state governments transcend the electoral cycle while the Union has no incentive to do so.

Self-interested politicians skewing the balance of power towards the chair they occupy is an unpleasant but inevitable consequence of representative democracy. In a federal union, especially one in which the Centre is much more powerful than the states, that means power invariably accrues in favour of the Union government.

This, in a country where development outcomes are so vastly divergent, ends up with perverse incentives for both policymaking and for situating the power of making that policy in the right layer of government. This is a well-known bug in many large federal unions, but the uniquely heterogeneous circumstances of India render this relatively common central power grab more dangerous. It could result in a slide towards making the Union itself unviable.

This tendency concentrates power in favour of the demographically mighty states that have done poorly and weakens those states that have done well. It punishes performance and rewards failure. Sooner or later, people in southern India will ask why the policy apparatus governing their health is lagging behind their lived reality by a generation and a half.

2

Education

Education: The Performance-enhancing Drug

Our ability to read, write and do arithmetic gives us the luxury of thinking better about our own lives and that of our fellow citizens. The transformative power of education is hard to overstate; it results in better health, increased happiness, greater material progress and a more stable society.

Democracy, more than any other form of governance, also depends on an educated and enlightened citizenry. This isn't new; Aristotle defined being well educated as the ability to discern in each subject which arguments belong to it and which are foreign to it. This ability is what helps one distinguish between good and bad policy or between candidates in a democracy. No reasonable person, therefore, would dispute the centrality of education in achieving our potential.

India – and several Asian countries – entered the twentieth century with their populations largely illiterate.

Broad-based formal education in the modern sense hadn't been introduced in these countries. Japan, following the Meiji restoration, was the only exception. Japan's success in making education universal and the positive impact that had on the country's economy in the late nineteenth and early twentieth centuries is a lesson many Asian and even European peers wanted to emulate.

Korea, Malaysia, Indonesia, Sri Lanka, Vietnam and China – all had poor literacy rates in the early twentieth century, just like India. But they caught up with Japan in varying ways, to varying degrees and with varying efficiency. All these countries now have near-universal literacy rates. India, sadly, still lags behind significantly, even in the twenty-first century. This gap shows up in other related metrics for the country too – India lags behind its Asian peers in health, manufacturing activity and per capita income.

Literacy rate, the most basic metric for measuring education, is a crude measure, just like life expectancy is for health. It's a lagging indicator and its accuracy is suspect as tests of literacy are poorly administered. The reported rates of literacy are often higher than the ground reality. Nevertheless, it is useful as a base measure of educational achievement, in that we can treat it as a necessary criterion. India as a whole had a literacy rate of 77.7 per cent in 2018. It had set itself a target of 80 per cent for 2011, but the country still hasn't met that modest target a decade past the deadline. And the target in itself is lower than the global average for low- and middle-income countries.

Table 1: Literacy Rate – Ages 7 and Above

State	Literacy Rate (%)
Andhra Pradesh	66
Assam	86
Bihar	71
Gujarat	82
Haryana	80
Jharkhand	74
Karnataka	77
Kerala	96
Madhya Pradesh	74
Maharashtra	85
Odisha	77
Punjab	84
Rajasthan	70
Tamil Nadu	83
Telangana	73
Uttar Pradesh	73
West Bengal	81

Source: Household Social Consumption on Education in India, NSS 75th Round, July 2017–June 2018, National Sample Survey Office, Ministry of Statistics and Programme Implementation

Within India, as one would expect, there's significant variance across states (see Table 1). Kerala has been India's leader in this measure for decades. It has near universal literacy for most age groups. Its neighbour, Tamil Nadu, has near universal literacy for young adults and teens and a lower rate for older people, thus showing improvements in literacy in its more recent history.

After all, getting children to school and getting them to learn to read, write and be numerate are primary responsibilities of a state, the fulfilling of which shows up as improved literacy among younger population subgroups. Improving literacy among older adults through adult literacy programmes or other means is a far more difficult task.

Therefore, a good way to understand educational achievements through literacy rates in a developing country with low overall literacy is to treat the older population as the base on which the younger population makes improvements.

Getting Children to School

India lags behind most of its peers in basic literacy, as it does in health. This divergence in literacy is more complicated than a one-time measure reveals and needs an age-wise break-up for our understanding of the relative performance of each society. After all, the effect of building a school, staffing it well and retaining children in school to show up in the data for literacy takes a significantly long time. How do India's states perform in delivering these necessary input conditions for schooling and education?

Census 2011 gives an age-wise break-up of literacy that is disaggregated by state. It's a great tool to look at how India's states have approached literacy and what effect their policies have had on their populations. For instance, the state of Kerala stands out as the best state by some distance right through. Its seniors are as literate as the rest of India's overall population, which includes the very young (see Tables 2 and 3).

Table 2: Literacy Rate – Ages 80+

State	Literacy Rate (%)
Kerala	69
Tamil Nadu	42
Maharashtra	47
Karnataka	38
Andhra Pradesh	32
Gujarat	41
Haryana	26
Punjab	28
West Bengal	50
Madhya Pradesh	30
Odisha	40
Jharkhand	34
Rajasthan	22
Assam	40
Uttar Pradesh	35
Bihar	36

Source: Census 2011, Census Division, Office of the Registrar General and Census Commissioner, Ministry of Home Affairs

The state of West Bengal, which ranks second, right behind Kerala, for literacy among people above 80, occupies the ninth place among large states for literacy among children aged 10 to 14. This differential in ranking between literacy of the old and young shows West Bengal's governance as one

Table 3: Literacy Rate – Ages 10–14

State	Literacy Rate (%)
Kerala	99
Tamil Nadu	98
Maharashtra	96
Karnataka	95
Andhra Pradesh	94
Gujarat	94
Haryana	93
Punjab	93
West Bengal	93
Madhya Pradesh	92
Odisha	92
Jharkhand	90
Rajasthan	89
Assam	88
Uttar Pradesh	88
Bihar	83

Source: Census 2011, Census Division, Office of the Registrar General and Census Commissioner, Ministry of Home Affairs

that has slipped in the past seventy years. In Andhra Pradesh, the situation is the reverse; it ranks 12th in the 80+ age group and 5th in the 10–14 age group. Andhra Pradesh's progress and West Bengal's decline in relative terms across age groups tell a far more compelling story than the literacy ranking for the entire population of the two states.

An even better way to understand this relative performance is to plot the two sets of data against each other – that is, the literacy rate of the 80+ age group against the literacy rate of the 10–14 age group – to understand how well or how poorly each state has performed. The resultant graph (Chart 1) reveals that Tamil Nadu, Karnataka and Andhra Pradesh are the states showing the most improvement, by virtue of having the largest positive residuals or showing the best performance relative to their base position. Bihar ranks last, with the largest negative residual or worst performance relative to its base.

Uttar Pradesh and Assam also have large negative residuals, pointing to poor performance. It is particularly noteworthy that Tamil Nadu, Maharashtra and Gujarat are peers in terms of literacy rate for the 80+ age group; but for

Chart 1: Literacy Rate Change – Ages 80+ vs 10–14

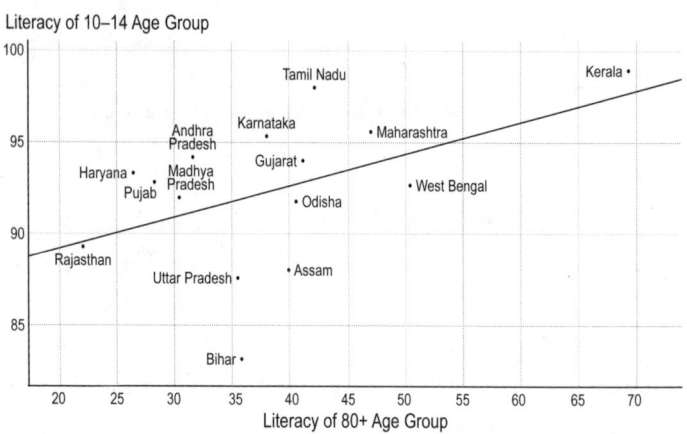

Note: Regression between the literacy rates of age groups 80+ and 10–14. A positive residual (states above the line) shows better than trend line performance over time. A negative residual (states below the line) shows less than expected performance. Tamil Nadu has shown the best performance and Bihar the worst.
Source: Census 2011, Census Division, Office of the Registrar General and Census Commissioner, Ministry of Home Affairs

the 10–14 age group, Tamil Nadu has broken out of this peer group and joined Kerala in attaining near universal literacy. Karnataka and the erstwhile unified state of Andhra Pradesh are the next best states in terms of improvement in literacry, as the chart indicates. Southern India, in other words, has outperformed India by some distance.

In a scenario where basic literacy is not yet universal, access to education becomes a crucial yardstick of progress. This is particularly true given the context of caste prejudice and discrimination that made such access uneven across society for much of history. A basic metric that measures access to education is the gross enrolment ratio (GER) – where we express the total number of enrolled students as a ratio of the overall population of children in that age group.

For example, the total number of children enrolled in primary schools expressed as a ratio of the total number of children who are in the age group where they ought to be attending primary school is the gross enrolment ratio for primary school. The numerator here includes repeaters and those who enrol late; thus it is possible for this ratio to exceed 100 per cent for the lower grades because older children are sometimes sent to school late. But, over time and grades, this ratio evens out and is a useful measure to understand how many children are attending school and, more importantly, how many are left out.

In recent years, most state governments in India have done a good job in getting children enrolled at the pre-primary, primary and upper primary levels. The GER for these levels is near universal for most states. This shows up in the high literacy rates among the very young for most states. It's the ability to keep these children in school as they progress to secondary and higher secondary levels that's a challenge for much of India. Some states do a better job than others in these next levels of measure (see Tables 4 and 5).

Table 4: GER, Secondary, 2016–17

State	GER
Andhra Pradesh	76
Assam	79
Bihar	77
Chhattisgarh	88
Gujarat	75
Haryana	86
Jharkhand	64
Karnataka	84
Kerala	99
Madhya Pradesh	80
Maharashtra	92
Odisha	80
Punjab	87
Rajasthan	77
Tamil Nadu	94
Telangana	82
Uttar Pradesh	68
West Bengal	79

Source: Department of Higher Education, Statistics Division, Ministry of Human Resource Development

Table 5: GER, Higher Secondary, 2016–17

State	GER
Andhra Pradesh	61
Assam	40
Bihar	29
Chhattisgarh	54
Gujarat	43
Haryana	61
Jharkhand	37
Karnataka	42
Kerala	79
Madhya Pradesh	47
Maharashtra	71
Odisha	40
Punjab	72
Rajasthan	60
Tamil Nadu	84
Telangana	51
Uttar Pradesh	59
West Bengal	51

Source: Department of Higher Education, Statistics Division, Ministry of Human Resource Development

GERs for secondary and higher secondary levels thus work as a real measure of the robustness of a state's basic education policy and its implementation. Firstly, they measure the ability of a state to keep children in school right from the primary stage. After all, a child needs to have gone through the previous grades to enrol into a higher grade. Secondly, to some degree, it's a measure of educational outcomes in the earlier grades too.

Students drop out of school owing to a variety of reasons. Sometimes, it is because of consistently low scores in exams. Sometimes, failure to get promoted to the next grade is the proximate cause. Fear of sexual violence and lack of safety are common reasons why teenaged girls discontinue school. Extreme poverty, bleak economic prospects and the opportunity cost of lost earnings of the child are other common reasons.

Thus, keeping children in school is often the result of overall good governance. Preventing discontinuation of school by students involves aspects of school education, general welfare policies and the ability to provide safety. It is both a lead indicator of progress and a lag indicator of governance, as well as an example of a virtuous circle. That is, students need a well-functioning society to stay in school, and their staying in school helps to build a better society in turn.

Data from the Ministry of Human Resource Development shows that Tamil Nadu and Kerala are the leaders in getting children to school and keeping them there till they reach higher grades. Maharashtra is the only other state to have over 90 per cent GER at secondary school levels. Kerala has had high enrolment ratios at all school levels for over two generations; Tamil Nadu, however, did not have such high enrolment rates historically, but in recent times, Tamil Nadu has, remarkably, even overtaken Kerala in the all-important GER measures for higher secondary schooling.

Tamil Nadu had a GER of 84 per cent for higher secondary schooling in 2016–17, whereas the corresponding figure for Kerala was 79 per cent. This is even more impressive given that this achievement by Tamil Nadu was on the back of a slightly lower GER for secondary school, at 94 per cent, lower than Kerala's 99 per cent. That is, Kerala suffers a 20 percentage point drop between secondary and higher secondary enrolments while Tamil Nadu has stemmed that drop to 10 percentage points. The goals for states should be to both raise GER at all levels and reduce the drop-off from one level to the next.

Chart 2: GER, Secondary vs Higher Secondary

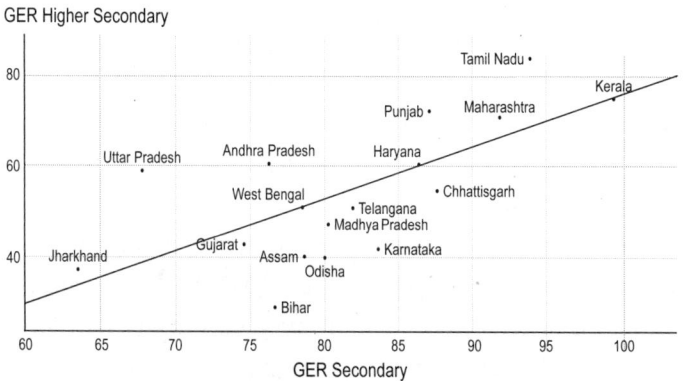

Note: Plot of GER in Secondary Level vs GER in Higher Secondary Level (2016–17). A positive residual from a higher base shows better governance.
Source: Department of Higher Education, Statistics Division, Ministry of Human Resource Development

As in the case of measuring literacy rate improvements, plotting of GERs for two school segments – secondary and higher secondary – against each other (see Chart 2) informs us how well a state is doing relative to its base. That is, taking as a base the number of students the state managed to get into secondary school, the graph tells us how well the state does in getting them to enrol into higher secondary school. As in the case of base literacy improvements, Tamil Nadu does very well, with a large positive residual despite a high base. Again, the state seems to break away from its peer, Maharashtra, and join Kerala, this time doing even better than Kerala. Similarly, Punjab and Haryana, two similar states that share a border and a capital, seem to have diverged, with Punjab doing significantly better than Haryana.

Getting Youth to College

GER is an even more important parameter in assessing higher education – i.e., enrolment into colleges, universities, professional courses and vocational streams.

India had an overall GER of 26 per cent in 2018–19 for higher education. Tamil Nadu, with a GER of 49 per cent in this category for that year, outperformed India and all its large states. It outperforms not just the large states, it outperforms even New Delhi, a city-state and an educational hub (see Table 6).

Table 6: GER, Higher Education

State	GER
Andhra Pradesh	32
Assam	19
Bihar	14
Chhattisgarh	19
Delhi	46
Gujarat	20
Haryana	29
Himachal Pradesh	40
Jharkhand	19
Karnataka	29
Kerala	37
Madhya Pradesh	22
Maharashtra	32
Odisha	22
Punjab	30
Rajasthan	23
Tamil Nadu	49
Telangana	36
Uttar Pradesh	26
West Bengal	19

Source: AISHE [All India Survey on Higher Education] Report 2018–19, Ministry of Human Resource Development, Department of Higher Education, 2019

That the state of Tamil Nadu – a large state with a vast rural hinterland – has a GER in higher education that's greater than that of a city that's also the national capital is a measure of remarkable progress. Kerala, Telangana and Andhra Pradesh are the other large states that follow Tamil

Nadu in this metric. This skew towards the southern states in higher education is a trend that was predictable, given their achievements in GER for the lower school grades.

GER in higher education, much like GER in higher secondary education, measures how well children are retained in school across every single grade. Secondly, it's a measure of the educational output of those previous levels. That is, if a university or some tertiary institution accepts students from school, it's a stamp of approval for their school education. Thirdly, and perhaps most importantly, it measures how much society values education. And finally, it points to a young college-educated workforce, which is predictive of higher economic growth and greater per capita income.

GER in higher education, therefore, is often cited as a metric for comparing developing countries. If one were to do that, India (27.1 per cent), in its entirety, ranks just above Botswana (25.1 per cent), but the southern states rank alongside Brazil (55 per cent) and China (58 per cent). Even India's best states still have some catching up to do with the OECD countries (76 per cent), while the rest have a lot more ground to cover.[1]

Come to Eat, Stay to Learn

It is clear from the data that getting children to school and retaining them there at the secondary and higher secondary levels is a crucial indicator of good governance. Consequently, the way in which states get children into school and prevent their dropping out has been a subject of policy experimentation and serious study for a century now.

The most improved state on this measure, Tamil Nadu, for instance, attributes much of its success in improving GER and curbing dropout rates to its pioneering midday meal scheme (see Table 7). The rationale that poor students will come to school to eat and will stay to learn has been a powerful touchstone of Tamil politics.

Table 7: Students Receiving Free Midday Meals (Among Those Who Attend Government Institutions)

State	Pre-Primary (%)	Primary School (%)	Middle School (%)	Secondary School (%)
Andhra Pradesh	97.3	98.8	97.0	86.9
Assam	86.3	94.9	81.6	10.8
Bihar	96.6	97.4	75.8	10.5
Chhattisgarh	95.1	99.3	93.7	8.6
Gujarat	97.0	98.0	88.6	11.0
Haryana	96.8	96.5	89.8	10.7
Himachal Pradesh	92.9	96.7	87.4	6.2
Jharkhand	96.8	97.7	90.0	11.4
Karnataka	100.0	98.4	98.6	92.8
Kerala	77.9	92.3	94.0	43.2
Madhya Pradesh	90.1	96.6	86.1	13.1
Maharashtra	95.3	96.5	81.8	24.3
Odisha	97.6	97.3	90.7	7.8
Punjab	97.3	92.8	76.5	9.5
Rajasthan	91.6	98.6	90.2	5.5

State	Pre-Primary (%)	Primary School (%)	Middle School (%)	Secondary School (%)
Tamil Nadu	87.5	94.8	91.3	85.4
Telangana	97.0	99.7	99.9	97.5
Uttarakhand	43.4	93.9	82.5	2.3
Uttar Pradesh	93.2	95.4	85.6	10.4
West Bengal	96.9	98.7	93.5	15.7

Source: NSS Report No. 585: Household Social Consumption on Education in India, NSS 75th Round, July 2017–June 2018, Ministry of Statistics and Programme Implementation, National Statistical Office

In 1923, after the Montagu–Chelmsford Reforms which allowed self-governance at the state and local levels in the colonial administration, Sir Pitti Theagaraya Chetty, the then president of the Madras Corporation Council and a founding member of the Justice Party, launched a free midday meal scheme for students in the city. It was a novel idea that sought to test the assumption that children would come for the food and stay for learning. However, it was discontinued by the British administration citing lack of funds a few years later.

The next iteration of it came after Independence, in 1956, when Tamil Nadu Chief Minister K. Kamaraj launched another version of the scheme. This was extended across the entire state and covered one-third of enrolled students for 200 days a year. The state government split the financial burden of this scheme with the local bodies. While this scheme brought in children living in far-flung areas to school, it saw uneven implementation, given its cost-sharing formula.

In 1982, Chief Minister M.G. Ramachandran relaunched the scheme to cover all children – initially in the rural areas, then later in the urban areas too – with the state bearing the entire financial burden. At the time of its launch, the scheme was generally considered fiscally profligate and unsustainable, given the enormous costs involved. But the state government went ahead and created an entire bureaucracy to administer and monitor its implementation.

Future chief ministers not only kept the scheme alive, but also actively added to it – such as including eggs and milk in the menu – making the noon meal scheme a defining aspect of Tamil Nadu's education policy. The proof of that 'bowl of rice' is evident in the state topping the GER charts a generation later.

This policy was so successful that the Supreme Court of India made it compulsory for all states to serve school children a midday meal in 2001. That bit of judicial activism in policy implementation has had mixed results. But, overall, in the years since that judgement, enrolment rates for primary school have improved. The southern states, which instituted similar schemes relatively early, learning from their neighbour even before this judicial intervention, still lead in implementation. The correlation between GER and midday meal coverage is apparent, still.

Karnataka stands out as a bit of a disappointment among its southern peers. For a state that has otherwise had good outcomes in literacy and basic schooling over the past few decades, its ability to retain children at the higher secondary level vis-à-vis secondary level is among the worst in the country. What's worse, the state, embroiled in political controversy, sought to keep students out of schools for reasons such as their clothing, or sought to tinker with the midday meal menus for religious reasons. For a state that isn't doing as well as it could, or should, this is particularly counterproductive.

Girls in school

The role of the midday meal and other incentivization programmes in enhancing GER and helping arrest dropout rates is now accepted wisdom. But it also had another benefit – it bridged the gap between the GERs for girls and boys. It also brought in those who were least likely to attend school – girls from poor and backward regions and from marginalized sections of society.

Dropout rates for girls are higher than for boys at all levels all across India, except in Kerala. Unsurprisingly, therefore, female literacy lags behind male literacy.

Keeping girls in school, however, is the greatest force multiplier for improving development outcomes. Education among girls is the most significant variable correlated with low fertility rates worldwide. It also results in a higher female labour force participation rate (LFPR).

Moreover, if and when an educated girl does become a parent, her own children will almost certainly be as educated as she is. It produces a virtuous cycle of fewer newborns, who have access to better basic health services, better education and higher per capita income.

When M.G. Ramachandran relaunched the midday meal scheme in Tamil Nadu, he explicitly mentioned provision of nutrition for women and girls as an important consideration when he answered critics who had accused him of spending beyond the state's means. In a single generation, that policy paid back many times over.

A measure of success in girls' education – which is a good proxy for education in general – is the percentage of women who received ten or more years of schooling. NFHS-4 data suggests that Kerala leads in this metric, followed by Himachal Pradesh, Punjab and Tamil Nadu (see Table 8).

But, as with overall literacy, this metric again measures the number of educated women in the overall population. Younger women making greater progress is a more reliable indicator of more recent gains. So, if we look at the improvements in the percentage of women who had over ten years of schooling between 2006 and 2016, predictably, southern India leads (see Table 9).

An important question for policymakers, given the context, is this: over and above the basic midday meal scheme and establishment of a school network that children can access, what makes girls stay in school?

Table 8: Women with More than 10 Years of Schooling

State	Women (%)
Andhra Pradesh	34
Assam	26
Bihar	23
Chhattisgarh	27
Gujarat	33
Haryana	46
Himachal Pradesh	59
Jammu and Kashmir	37
Jharkhand	29
Karnataka	46
Kerala	72
Madhya Pradesh	23
Maharashtra	42
Odisha	27
Punjab	55
Rajasthan	25
Tamil Nadu	51
Telangana	31
Uttar Pradesh	33
West Bengal	27

Source: National Family Health Survey (NFHS-4), 2015–16: India, International Institute for Population Sciences, 2017

It turns out that girls often drop out of school in the higher secondary stages because of concerns over menstrual hygiene, availability of toilets in school, etc. States where

Table 9: Improvement in Women with 10 Years of Schooling, 2006–2016

State	*Absolute Improvement (Measures Improvement in % Point Terms)*
Kerala	24
Tamil Nadu	19
Karnataka	18
Punjab	17
Haryana	16
Himachal Pradesh	15
Uttar Pradesh	15
Chhattisgarh	14
Jharkhand	14
Rajasthan	13
Maharashtra	11
Odisha	11
West Bengal	11
Jammu and Kashmir	11
Bihar	10
Gujarat	10
Madhya Pradesh	9
Assam	7

Source: National Family Health Survey (NFHS-4), 2015–16: India, International Institute for Population Sciences, 2017

girls and women have greater access to menstrual hygiene are, generally, also states where they stay longer in school (Chart 3).

Chart 3: Access to Menstrual Hygiene vs Women Staying in School

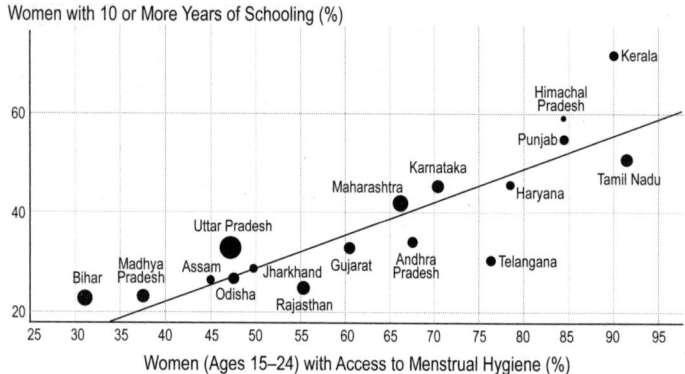

Note: Size of circles scaled by population of each state
Source: *National Family Health Survey (NFHS-4), 2015–16: India*, International Institute for Population Sciences, 2017

Southern India leads when it comes to the metric of availability and access to menstrual hygiene for women in the 15–24 age group, just as it leads in the improvement in percentage of girls with ten years of schooling (see Table 10). This buttresses its GER in higher secondary education and improvement in literacy of younger populations as well.

Table 10: Women (Ages 15–24) with Access to Menstrual Hygiene

State	Women of Ages 15–24 with Access (%)
Andhra Pradesh	68
Assam	45
Bihar	31

State	Women of Ages 15–24 with Access (%)
Chhattisgarh	47
Gujarat	60
Haryana	78
Himachal Pradesh	84
Jammu and Kashmir	67
Jharkhand	50
Karnataka	70
Kerala	90
Madhya Pradesh	37
Maharashtra	66
Odisha	47
Punjab	84
Rajasthan	55
Tamil Nadu	91
Telangana	76
Uttar Pradesh	47
West Bengal	55

Source: National Family Health Survey (NFHS-4), 2015–16: India, International Institute for Population Sciences, 2017

India's Centralizing Approach to Education

Southern Indian states – particularly Kerala and Tamil Nadu – have a system where almost every child gets into primary school and where about eight in ten stay on and get to higher secondary school. In Tamil Nadu's case, one out of every two young people get a tertiary education of some sort. Telangana, Andhra Pradesh and Karnataka are states that are fast improving too.

Meanwhile, states such as Gujarat, Madhya Pradesh, Rajasthan and Uttar Pradesh diverge significantly from their southern counterparts in both absolute values and trends. Even with a higher achievement base, Tamil Nadu and Kerala are accelerating faster. This makes it necessary for education policy in the southern states to move to the next level, going beyond the monitoring of basic input measures such as GER to making changes to pedagogy and syllabi.

States like Gujarat that have steep dropout rates in the transition from secondary to higher secondary levels should ideally focus on gender parity and other targeted aspects that will result in lower dropout rates among teenagers. Still other states – particularly those in central and northern India – where dropouts happen from upper primary to secondary levels, should probably take an entirely different approach, which will have more to do with expansion of access and possible incentive mechanisms to get children to come to school.

Each state thus needs an education policy that is tailored to its needs. A single policy is inefficient and maybe impossible to achieve, given that the needs of different states are often at odds with each other. But, more importantly, optimizing policy for all states in such a scenario, where the states' higher secondary GERs range from OECD levels to sub-Saharan Africa levels, means no state will really benefit. The policy will be variously too expensive, or too negligent, or not sufficiently inclusive for each individual state. Every reasonable onlooker would agree that the only path forward is for states to decide their own education policies.

The NEP of 2020, unveiled by the Government of India, went the opposite way instead. It recommends a single policy for all of India that ends up, as one feared, comically bureaucratic in terms of its details and absurdly bombastic in terms of its political intent. The document sets India a target of 50 per cent GER in higher education by 2035. Tamil Nadu's GER, as seen already, was 49 per cent in 2018.

The incongruity of this target alone is emblematic of how unfeasible the policy is. The NEP document further lays emphasis on uniform standardized testing as a strategy to measure educational outcome and as an admission criterion across all states, for various stages. Firstly, there are school-level exams proposed for classes three, five and eight that are designed to test educational outcomes at those levels.

With a GER that drops significantly at the secondary and higher secondary levels in many states, testing students at these crucial stages will only make the problem worse in those states.

Would we as a society rather have children drop out of class five because they failed an exam or stay on despite their not having achieved the desired outcome levels?

The answer, in a society where there are high dropout numbers, is that perhaps we'd rather have the child stay on in school. Kerala and Tamil Nadu, though, may now take the risk of facing a higher dropout metric given their relatively high GER. But whatever the choice, that decision is one that the state governments are supposed to be making, taking into account their societies' priorities. It is why we elect state governments.

The NEP 2020 further lays out a plan to have a national testing agency for admission into tertiary colleges and universities all across the country. These are colleges and universities in different states that run their education programmes differently from each other, with each of them having different social priorities and being in divergent stages of evolution.

The focus of the syllabi and pedagogy at the schools that feed students into these tertiary institutions is all very different. What these tests achieve, if anything, is to sort students on one scale. That scale is irrelevant at best and likely dangerous at worst because it too belongs in a context, and that context may be alien to the states' own contexts.

Standardized tests, such as the ones proposed by the NEP and those that are in use globally, have been found to have serious issues.[2] When used as an entrance criterion for college admission, they are found to be poor predictors of student success. After all, if an entrance test is supposed to measure merit, it should, with its score, be able to reasonably predict how well the student actually performs in the course which he or she is admitted to. This isn't true for standardized tests, globally. It's been found that students' aggregate grades/exam scores in the past years – in whatever system of education they belonged to – are a better predictor.[3]

Standardized tests also have the additional undesirable effect of reflecting the existing social inequities in their scores. Globally, therefore, there's a move away from these tests as a criterion for admission into colleges and universities.[4] India, meanwhile, seems intent on hurtling towards a discredited idea in search of a unified policy solution that doesn't exist.

An example of such a single national testing strategy is the NEET for admission to undergraduate medical courses in all medical institutions in India. This has already been made mandatory for all states. State governments run their own health systems; consequently, they also run most of the large teaching hospitals that train the doctors who eventually people these systems. Private institutions in these states are also regulated by state governments. This meant that until recently, states had the ability to run programmes and determine entry criteria for medical education that suited their educational and health profiles.

Successful states, such as Tamil Nadu, had built capacity that far exceeded the country's per capita average in terms of doctors. They also ran their incentive programmes that offered doctors preference in the admission programmes in advanced fields in exchange for rural service. Tamil Nadu also had a higher proportion of seats reserved for the oppressed sections of society than the rest of India in its college admission process. More crucially, the state did not have a standardized entrance test for its medical colleges.

These factors meant that more students from a wider socio-economic base were admitted to medical colleges in Tamil Nadu and trained to become doctors. There's evidence from several studies that doctors who belong to the same social background as patients help achieve better health outcomes in those communities.[5] The record of health outcomes in Tamil Nadu is proof of how well those students – picked from a wider social base and based on their performance in school – did as doctors, as the data in the previous section shows.

To take another example, Karnataka has the highest capacity for training doctors and would want to use that capacity to improve its own health outcomes first. The NEET regime restricts the ability of the state to do that and instead seeks to optimize medical education for the entire country, thus disincentivizing capacity-building in a specific state while distributing some of the capacity that's already been built in one state across all states. The states that have built capacity and run specific programmes in health and education to create a pipeline of doctors now have a regime that taxes their success.

Successful states that ran incentive programmes to suit their individual situations find themselves in a nationwide zero-sum game.

The NEP 2020 imagines an admission process similar to NEET for all disciplines. The relentless pursuit of homogeneity has only accelerated over time. Education was originally a state subject. This was moved to the concurrent list in 1976 as part of the 42nd Amendment Act of 1976, passed during the Emergency. Since then, every government at the Centre has been increasing the role of the Union government in education. Invariably, all of these attempts have also been steps towards centralizing education in terms of syllabi and pedagogy.

The three-language formula for schools is an example of India's centralizing thrust. In various overt and covert ways, the Government of India has been trying to get Hindi taught in schools, at least since 1968 when the policy was adopted by Parliament. It's an old project of the Government of India to emphasize Hindi as a tool of integration.

No reasonable person would object to the learning of a third language if it is of a student's own volition. But in India, where not enough children get to school and even when they do, not enough of them learn to read and write in any language, a third language is a waste of precious class time – especially when it's mandated and the choice of that language is restricted. After protests against imposition of Hindi, the NEP 2020's final version removed references to Hindi that were in the draft version, but still prescribes a three-language formula that emphasizes preference for 'Indian languages' in general, and Sanskrit in particular.

The idea of an 'Indian language' is an invented political category that linguists would not recognize. There are Indo-European languages, to which Sanskrit, Hindi and the many languages spoken in the Indo-Gangetic plains belong. Then there are Dravidian languages, such as Tamil,

Telugu, Kannada, Malayalam and others, spoken largely in southern India. Some languages that are spoken in the east and north-east of the country belong to the Sino-Tibetan family of languages.

All this makes one wonder what an Indian language is. Is it one that's spoken within what are today the political boundaries of India? In which case, English would count as an Indian language. Is it one that originated in what is today India? In which case, Sanskrit, which originated in Central Asia, doesn't qualify. Is it one that originated in India and is also spoken in India? In which case, both English and Sanskrit would get thrown out.

The three-language formula has nothing to do with education policy and everything to do with politics. And given that it's a political decision, the opposing reaction to it, again, is deeply political. That is why Tamil Nadu, the state with a history of anti-Hindi agitation, has opposed the three-language formula in its most recent iteration too.

Table 11: Distribution of Medium of Instruction in Primary Schools

Language	Medium of Instruction Same as Language Spoken at Home (%)	English as the Medium of Instruction (%)
Hindi	60	38
Assamese	74	24
Bengali	75	18

Language	Medium of Instruction Same as Language Spoken at Home (%)	English as the Medium of Instruction (%)
Bodo	23	23
Gujarati	71	27
Kannada	42	53
Malayalam	19	81
Manipuri	18	68
Marathi	55	43
Nepali	2	75
Odiya	81	17
Punjabi	20	78
Tamil	9	91
Telugu	17	80
Urdu	6	82

Note: Only language with >1 per cent attendance in same language instruction are considered – as a result, Sanskrit, Konkani, Dogri, Kashmiri, etc., have been left out.

Source: NSS Report No. 585: Household Social Consumption on Education in India, NSS 75th Round, July 2017–June 2018, Ministry of Statistics and Programme Implementation, National Statistical Office

The other deeply problematic aspect of the NEP's language policy is that it wants students to learn their school subjects in their mother tongue and not English. An overwhelming proportion of children in southern India choose English as their medium of instruction (see Table 11). Given that English is the global language in which cutting-edge knowledge gets disseminated first, it's become the preferred option in states that have high GER. These states also happen to be non-Hindi-speaking states. The idea of imposing a three-language formula that may result in children not becoming very fluent in English by not offering it to them as the medium of instruction only stokes the paranoia among non-Hindi-speaking states that this is an attempt by the government to replace English with Hindi as the default and dominant link language.

The glorification of Sanskrit – a language that's been dead for all practical purposes for several centuries – in the NEP and an insistence on learning it is another problematic area for parts of the country that do not speak Indo-European languages and for religious communities that aren't Hindu.

People learn new languages for one among the following reasons: there's either economic value in learning them, or they want to assimilate into a community, or they want to explore the lived experience of people who speak that language through its literature, or there's cutting-edge research that happens in that language. Sanskrit doesn't check any of these boxes – which makes the NEP's insistence on it problematic.

India, according to the Economic Survey for 2018–19 released by the country's finance ministry, spent 3.1 per cent of its GDP on education. This is a combined expenditure figure for both the state and central governments and is an extremely low ratio compared with those of the world's leading countries, and even many of the struggling ones.

The Union government also lays out, through its centrally sponsored flagship schemes in education, much of the state's education expenditure choices. The states already have very little fiscal room, given India's tax collection skew that favours the central government, and expenditure skew, which burdens the states. Taken together, it appears the Union government is using allocation of tax revenue as a bargaining chip for states to agree to the centralizing policy regime in education.

People pursue education for a wide variety of purposes. Commonly, they seek status, or money, or both. Sometimes they seek knowledge to achieve some specific goal. On rare occasions, it's for knowledge for its own sake. Whatever the purpose of individuals seeking education, liberal societies generally look to expand access to education for as many people as possible. The hope is that as expansion of access to education is a good thing in itself, it really doesn't matter what the individual's motivations are.

Another assumption in liberal societies is that expansion of access to education does a better job of achieving excellence than sorting and filtering the best into limited capacities. Some societies, on the other hand, may decide they'd rather filter and pick their best and pack them into elite places. This is an illiberal choice, but a choice nonetheless. The problem with India's increasing centralization is that it robs states of that choice to pick what suits them depending on where they are and who they are. This is as true of basic school systems – where the NEP and flagship projects seek to centralize school education – as it is for higher education, where the Union government wants a national standardized testing framework to be the basis for all admissions.

3

Economy

It's Still the Economy, Stupid

India's states are unlike each other in the extreme. Haryana, one of India's richest states, is six times richer than Bihar. In the years shortly after Independence, West Bengal was richer than most other large states in India when measured on a per capita income basis. Maharashtra, Punjab and Gujarat were close behind. In the last six decades, though, West Bengal has fallen significantly off its pole position; it is now a low-income state even by Indian standards. The rest of the high-income states on the list mentioned above have remained relatively stable. The distance between the rich and poor states, nevertheless, has widened. All five of the southern states, unsurprisingly, were among the ten richest large states in 2018–19.

A prevailing theory in newly independent India was that with time, the economic growth and per capita income of various states would converge. This hypothesis was one of the assumptions on which the centralized approach to industrial planning was anchored back then. But many researchers have now shown that economically disparate states do not converge to a single steady state.[1] They converge to different "steady" states, instead. That is, poor states converge to being poor; rich ones converge to being rich. Some reasonably well-to-do states have done better than their rich peers; and that, data suggests, can be entirely explained by state-level policymaking and implementation.

It is useful at this stage to take a step back and ask some key questions: What counts as a rich state in India? If one had a choice, is one better off being born in a state with a relatively high per capita income? Like, say, Gujarat? Or should one look for other markers of prosperity even if one were to restrict oneself to economic prospects as criterion? Also, why are the rich states rich and, conversely, why are the poor ones poor? What's the Union government's role in each state's economic trajectory? Does its policy even have an effect?

What should states do to ensure prosperity for their citizens? What can they do, and are they given the space in India's federal structure to do what they ought to be doing, to achieve this?

Agriculture: Source of India's Woes

Agriculture, which was the mainstay of the country's economic output at the time of Independence, has remained an unproductive and low-yielding economic activity for a variety of reasons. Despite that, it still employs the largest number of people in India. Subsistence farming has been a source and a symptom of poverty for a long time now. Economic progress in India and in much of the developing world, therefore, has been linked to moving people away from agriculture and into manufacturing and services.

No country became rich by growing food crops in the last half century, after all. Agriculture contributes less than 5 per cent to the GDP in most advanced economies. Agriculture has also been ruinous to India's environment, given the focus on hydrophilic crops such as paddy, wheat and sugarcane. These crops have minimum support prices (MSPs) that encourage their sowing at the expense of other crops which demand less water. The loss of crop diversity in the country has meant an overdependence on pesticides, which results in pesticide run-offs. Poor farming practices have thus contributed to desertifying an already water-starved country.

A good way to understand the economy of various states is to look at the different sectors and their respective contributions to the states. The degree of agriculture's contribution to the Gross State Domestic Product (GSDP) serves as a useful benchmark of a state's progress.

One may assume that states with a low agricultural output to GSDP ratio are on the path towards industrialization and modernization of their societies. This doesn't have to mean that those states have low agricultural output; rather, it is that their output in other sectors is high.

Interestingly, the states with high levels of human development and relative prosperity have the lowest contribution of agriculture towards their GSDP (see Table 1). For example, agriculture contributes only 3.91 per cent to Tamil Nadu's GSDP. That's the lowest proportion in the country among the large states. Kerala follows its neighbour, at 4.07 per cent. Other peninsular states, like Telangana, Maharashtra and Karnataka, all have relatively low ratios too. Among the southern states, only Andhra Pradesh has a double-digit ratio, with agriculture contributing 11.5 per cent to its GSDP.

Table 1: Levels of Agriculture to GSDP Ratio

Ratio of Gross State Value (GSV) added by agriculture and GSDP, for 2018–19. At constant prices. Base year 2011–12.

State	*Agriculture to GSDP Ratio*
Tamil Nadu	4
Kerala	4
Telangana	5
Maharashtra	5
Karnataka	5
Himachal Pradesh	6
Jharkhand	6
Gujarat	6
Odisha	7
Haryana	8
Chhattisgarh	10

State	Agriculture to GSDP Ratio
Bihar	11
Andhra Pradesh	11
Rajasthan	12
Assam	12
West Bengal	12
Uttar Pradesh	13
Punjab	13
Madhya Pradesh	21

Source: Handbook of Statistics on Indian States 2019–20, Reserve Bank of India

States with low human development indices and low per capita incomes, meanwhile, dominate the list of states where agriculture contributes significantly to the GSDP. Punjab is the exception to India's agriculture conundrum. It is a relatively prosperous state with reasonable levels of human development that still has a high degree of dependence on farming as an economic activity. Agriculture contributes 13.27 per cent to Punjab's GSDP. It's also the state with the highest yields per hectare, which makes farming a worthwhile profession there, unlike in most other states.

The problem of agriculture being poorly remunerative is a worldwide phenomenon. But in India, it is further complicated by the large numbers of people working on small tracts of land that yield harvests much below the global averages.

Table 2: Rice Yield, 2017–18

State	Rice Yield (kg/hectare)
West Bengal	2,926
Punjab	4,366
Uttar Pradesh	2,283
Andhra Pradesh	2,792
Bihar	2,409
Tamil Nadu	3,923
Odisha	1,765
Telangana	3,176
Assam	2,107
Chhattisgarh	1,256
Haryana	3,181
Madhya Pradesh	2,026

Source: *Agricultural Statistics at a Glance 2018*, Directorate of Economics and Statistics, Department of Agriculture, Cooperation and Farmers Welfare, Ministry of Agriculture and Farmers Welfare

Consider rice yields. The global average rice yield is about 4.25 metric tonnes per hectare (mt/ha). Only Punjab, with a yield of 4.3 mt/ha, does marginally better than that global average (see Table 2). Tamil Nadu, with 3.9 mt/ha, comes close. Every other state has a yield significantly lower than the global average. States like Madhya Pradesh, Odisha and Chhattisgarh have rice yields that are in the bottom quintile of global yields. Uttar Pradesh and Bihar, despite being geographically situated in the historically fertile Gangetic plains, don't have much better yields either.

Table 3: Wheat Yield, 2017–18

State	Wheat Yield (kg/hectare)
Uttar Pradesh	3,269
Punjab	5,090
Madhya Pradesh	2,993
Haryana	4,412
Rajasthan	3,270
Bihar	2,816
Gujarat	2,932
Maharashtra	1,761
Uttarakhand	2,727
Himachal Pradesh	1,734

Source: Ministry of Agriculture and Farmers Welfare, Government of India

The data showing yields for wheat paints a similar picture as well (see Table 3). It's only Punjab, with a yield of 5.09 mt/ha, that beats the global average of 4.63 mt/ha. Haryana, with a yield of 4.4 mt/ha, comes close to that global average while every other state lags behind. In maize production, Tamil Nadu, with 7.7 mt/ha, and Andhra Pradesh, with 6.8 mt/ha, beat the world average, while other states lag behind (see Table 4). The only crop where many states in India do better than the global average is sugarcane (see Table 5). The majority of the crops mentioned here, apart from being low-yielding, are also hydrophilic. For a country that's water deficient with a rapidly falling water table, this is not only bad economics but also a terrible environmental choice.

Table 4: Maize Yield, 2017–18

State	Maize Yield (kg/hectare)
Karnataka	2,755
Maharashtra	3,062
Madhya Pradesh	2,615
Tamil Nadu	7,744
Telangana	4,061
Bihar	3,623
Andhra Pradesh	6,851
Rajasthan	1,884
Uttar Pradesh	1,981
West Bengal	4,805

Source: Ministry of Agriculture and Farmers Welfare, Government of India

Table 5: Sugarcane Yield, 2017–18

State	Sugarcane Yield (kg/hectare)
Uttar Pradesh	79,255
Maharashtra	92,166
Karnataka	80,751
Tamil Nadu	92,002
Bihar	59,202
Gujarat	66,220
Haryana	84,500
Punjab	83,583
Andhra Pradesh	80,283
Uttarakhand	70,044
Madhya Pradesh	55,408
Telangana	73,086

Source: Ministry of Agriculture and Farmers Welfare, Government of India

The states that have agriculture contributing to a large part of their GSDP, counterintuitively, also have the lowest crop yields, with Punjab again being an exception. That is, not only do the poor states in India have agriculture making up a large portion of their economic output – implying poor industrialization – their yields are also among the poorest worldwide. Their poverty seems to contribute to low yields, which in turn seem to result in making people poorer still.

It's a vicious cycle that can only be broken by reducing the dependence on agriculture and moving a lot of people into higher-value economic activity. Those who wish to move must have the requisite education to get employment in an industrialized economy. This in turn, demands investments in health and education and early child development. It warrants policymaking that will bear fruit only after a generation. No politician or policymaker in the states scattered across the Indo-Gangetic plains seems to be working on that kind of time scale.

A useful data point to look at in this context, especially given the contribution of agriculture to each state's GSDP, is, how many households in rural parts of the state are classified as agricultural (see Table 6).

The broad trends show that Kerala (27 per cent) and Tamil Nadu (35 per cent) have the least proportion of rural households classified as agricultural (see Table 6). That is, not only is agriculture a very small part of the economy in Kerala and Tamil Nadu, significantly fewer people as a proportion of the rural population are dependent on it. This is true in

Table 6: Rural Households That Are Agricultural Households

State	Agricultural Households to Rural Households (%)
Andhra Pradesh	42
Assam	65
Bihar	51
Chhattisgarh	68
Gujarat	67
Haryana	61
Himachal Pradesh	67
Jharkhand	60
Karnataka	55
Kerala	27
Madhya Pradesh	71
Maharashtra	57
Odisha	58
Punjab	51
Rajasthan	78
Tamil Nadu	35
Telangana	52
Uttar Pradesh	75
West Bengal	45

Source: Situation Assessment Survey of Agricultural Households, January–December 2013, NSS 70th Round, National Sample Survey Organization, Ministry of Statistics and Programme Implementation (MOSPI), 2013

varying degrees across peninsular India too – fewer people depend on agriculture in the peninsular states than in the rest of India, while their agricultural output is also larger.

In contrast, Madhya Pradesh, Uttar Pradesh and Rajasthan have over 70 per cent of rural households classified as agricultural. These are also the states where yields are low, the overall production middling and the contribution of agriculture to GSDP high. It's reasonable, therefore, to think of agriculture as the occupation of last resort.

The states where dependence on agriculture is low are also states that are urbanized the most. Or conversely, those that do depend on agriculture are urbanized the least. That is, not only do states dependent on agriculture have a large proportion of their rural population working in the fields, they also have a large rural population.

Table 7: Urban Population (Census 2011)

State	2011 (%)
Andhra Pradesh	33
Assam	14
Bihar	11
Chhattisgarh	23
Gujarat	43
Haryana	35
Himachal Pradesh	10
Jharkhand	24
Karnataka	39
Kerala	48
Madhya Pradesh	28
Maharashtra	45
Odisha	17

State	2011 (%)
Punjab	37
Rajasthan	25
Tamil Nadu	48
Uttar Pradesh	22
West Bengal	32

Source: Census 2011, Census Division, Office of the Registrar General and Census Commissioner, Ministry of Home Affairs

Bihar, India's most large rural state, has only 11.29 per cent of its population classified as urban; Uttar Pradesh – a state of 200 million people – has just 22 per cent of its population classified as urban (see Table 7). Tamil Nadu, with 48.4 per cent of its population classified as urban in census 2011, was the most urbanized large state; Kerala followed closely behind, with 47.7 per cent. This trend is likely to be further accentuated in the 2021 Census, whenever that data is released.

There are fewer people in villages in the southern states, and even among those who have stayed back in the villages, a lower proportion depends on agriculture. Maharashtra, the other well-off state with relatively good metrics in health and education, follows the two southern states closely, with 45.22 per cent of its population classified as urban.

In contrast, the more populous states like Uttar Pradesh and Bihar have a large majority of their population classified as rural, within which the majority live in families that are classified as agricultural. The absolute population numbers dependent on agriculture are very large in these states. Looked at another way, the overall population of Uttar Pradesh is about three times that of Tamil Nadu, while the number of people who live in rural agricultural households in Uttar Pradesh is closer to ten times the number in the southern state. Or, a resident of Uttar Pradesh is three times more likely to depend on subsistence farming than a resident of one of the southern states.

India's Unemployment Crisis: Twenty-First-Century Hole in a Nineteenth-Century Crater

India's largest economic sector, agriculture is unproductive and unevenly productive across the states. It employs too many people, produces too little value and is environmentally destructive. Jobs in other sectors of the economy are thus crucial for any meaningful economic progress in India. Sadly, India has been in the midst of a job crisis in those very sectors for most of the twenty-first century.

In the first phase of this job crisis, the popular press called the phenomenon 'jobless growth'. Even those in government, such as the former prime minister, Dr Manmohan Singh, started using that term eventually while still in office. In the years since, economic growth faltered a bit and job growth has not even kept pace with population growth. There have been actual job losses among some cohorts in the past decade, which is especially concerning in a developing country with massive unemployment and underemployment.

Depending on how we count workers, between 2011–12 and 2017–18, a six-year period, there were between 10 million and 14 million jobs added, according to the Periodic Labour Force Survey (PLFS), 2018–19.[2] That's approximately 2 million jobs per year. For context, about 12.5 million college-educated people become eligible to join the workforce each year. There are likely four times that number who have never been to college, who become eligible to join the workforce. In other words, the number of new jobs added each year is a tiny fraction of the number that needs employment.

For a country that still has a growing population, this is a terrifying prospect. India has significantly more people wanting to join the workforce each year than in the previous year. In addition, the economy was nowhere near offering full employment to begin with; which means those already in the workforce are not sufficiently employed.

All of this points to what anybody travelling through India's small towns would notice: there are a large number of young people with no prospect of a job. If there's one factor that's common to societies that witnessed violent uprisings or revolutions, it's precisely this. This has been true for times as varied and as far apart as the French Revolution and the Arab Spring. India is staring at the prospect of such upheavals if it doesn't do something urgently on a dramatically vast scale.

Table 8: LFPR, 2018–19

State	Total (%)	Female (%)
Andhra Pradesh	64	45
Assam	49	14
Bihar	41	5
Chhattisgarh	67	52
Gujarat	55	24
Haryana	55	17
Himachal Pradesh	72	64
Jammu and Kashmir	59	36
Jharkhand	51	23
Karnataka	57	28
Kerala	55	35
Madhya Pradesh	57	30
Maharashtra	58	35
Odisha	55	27
Punjab	52	21
Rajasthan	57	34
Tamil Nadu	60	40
Telangana	60	42
Uttar Pradesh	44	14
West Bengal	55	24

Note: Total (rural + urban combined) according to usual status (PS+SS) for 15–59 age group
Source: Annual Report, Periodic Labour Force Survey (PLFS), July 2018–June 2019, Ministry of Statistics and Programme Implementation, National Statistical Office

The LFPR for states provides an overall summation of the situation (see Table 8). Demographers assume that the workforce consists of people aged between 15 and 60.

However, not all of them will be seeking employment. The ratio of those seeking employment to the entire workforce is known as the LFPR.

States like Bihar and Uttar Pradesh, despite having large populations and high TFRs, have the lowest LFPRs. Yet, strangely enough, they have much lower unemployment rates than richer and more urbanized states. Even though these states have many people, and few have found work, people do not call themselves unemployed. Not only are the young people in these states not working, many are not even looking for work.

Table 9: State-wise Number of Workers, 2017–18

State	No. of Workers
Andhra Pradesh	486,646
Assam	180,489
Bihar	104,057
Chhattisgarh	147,310
Gujarat	1,403,204
Haryana	674,373
Himachal Pradesh	146,633
Jharkhand	153,026
Karnataka	828,689
Kerala	241,789
Madhya Pradesh	281,063
Maharashtra	1,414,565
Odisha	229,036
Punjab	569,266

State	No. of Workers
Rajasthan	432,434
Tamil Nadu	2,095,223
Telangana	669,220
Uttar Pradesh	839,121
West Bengal	516,740

Source: Annual Survey of Industries (ASI) 2017–18, Central Statistics Office (Industrial Statistics Wing), Ministry of Statistics and Programme Implementation

Table 10: State-wise Total Persons Engaged, 2017–18

State	No. of Persons Engaged
Andhra Pradesh	597,292
Assam	217,155
Bihar	121,772
Chhattisgarh	185,805
Gujarat	1,826,748
Haryana	858,313
Himachal Pradesh	205,781
Jharkhand	192,282
Karnataka	1,065,346
Kerala	310,326
Madhya Pradesh	378,022
Maharashtra	2,007,794
Odisha	279,496
Punjab	708,232
Rajasthan	556,103
Tamil Nadu	2,523,483
Telangana	794,520

State	No. of Persons Engaged
Uttar Pradesh	1,070,841
West Bengal	663,751

Source: Annual Survey of Industries (ASI) 2017–18, Central Statistics Office (Industrial Statistics Wing), Ministry of Statistics and Programme Implementation

Consider the industrialized states like Maharashtra, Tamil Nadu, Gujarat, et al. A natural corollary to their having a low contribution of agriculture to their GSDPs is a better mix of manufacturing, services and industry contributing towards their respective GSDPs. Since those other sectors, particularly manufacturing and industries, are more productive than agriculture, their contribution to the economy is much larger than agriculture, even though they employ only a fraction of the people that agriculture does.

Table 11: Manufacturing to GSDP Ratio

State	Manufacturing to GSDP (%)
Gujarat	32.6
Himachal Pradesh	29.9
Tamil Nadu	22.0
Haryana	21.0
Odisha	20.5
Maharashtra	20.3
Jharkhand	19.8

State	Manufacturing to GSDP (%)
Karnataka	16.5
Uttar Pradesh	16.3
Assam	15.3
Chhattisgarh	14.5
West Bengal	14.4
Punjab	13.7
Telangana	12.3
Kerala	11.8
Rajasthan	11.8
Madhya Pradesh	11.1
Andhra Pradesh	10.3
Bihar	8.8

Note: Ratio of Gross State Value added by manufacturing and Gross State Domestic Product, for 2018–19. At constant prices. Base year 2011–12.
Source: Handbook of Statistics on Indian States 2019–20, Reserve Bank of India

The standard path out of subsistence farming and into the middle-income category for countries that did not find massive oil wealth beneath their ground has been through manufacturing. The economists' dogma is that only the manufacturing sector can generate enough jobs for the vast numbers of people that India has been employing in subsistence agriculture. This is now the conventional wisdom. The overall contribution of manufacturing to GSDP, therefore, is a useful metric to track.

States that have done well on this count are likely to generate better-paying manufacturing jobs and move more citizens to middle-income levels. An even more important set of metrics is the total number of factories per state and the actual number of people employed. A single large automated factory, or an oil refinery owned by a very large company, can generate a lot of value and skew the contribution of manufacturing to GSDP, but it probably doesn't generate as much employment as a series of smaller factories, for instance.

According to the Reserve Bank of India, Gujarat topped the list of states ranked in terms of the share of manufacturing to their GSDP, at 32.59 per cent for 2017–18 (see Table 11). Tamil Nadu ranked second, at 22 per cent, and had the most number of factories, at 37,787, significantly more than Gujarat, which had 26,586 factories (see Table 12).

Table 12: State-wise Number of Factories, 2017–18

State	No. of Factories
Andhra Pradesh	16,296
Assam	4,538
Bihar	3,461
Chhattisgarh	3,352
Gujarat	26,586
Haryana	8,891
Himachal Pradesh	2,671
Jharkhand	2,866
Karnataka	13,518
Kerala	7,649

State	No. of Factories
Madhya Pradesh	4,533
Maharashtra	26,393
Odisha	3,066
Punjab	12,726
Rajasthan	9,212
Tamil Nadu	37,787
Telangana	15,263
Uttar Pradesh	15,830
West Bengal	9,534

Source: Annual Survey of Industries (ASI), Ministry of Statistics and Programme Implementation

Consequently, Tamil Nadu also has the maximum number of workers employed for any state, at over 2 million. Maharashtra and Gujarat both have roughly the same number of factories and employ approximately the same number of workers (about 1.4 million each).

Another true measure of job creation in manufacturing or other sectors is how demand for labour gets reflected in the wages of general agricultural and non-agricultural labour. If there is real demand for skilled and semi-skilled labour, then one could reasonably expect even the wages for unskilled labour to show a little buoyancy. Kerala has the highest wage rates for both (see Tables 13 and 14).

Table 13: Average Average Daily Wage Rates for Men in Rural India (Non-agricultural Labourers), 2019–20

State	Average Daily Wage (INR)
Andhra Pradesh	291
Assam	264
Bihar	267
Gujarat	234
Haryana	376
Himachal Pradesh	343
Karnataka	264
Kerala	670
Madhya Pradesh	206
Maharashtra	240
Odisha	241
Punjab	332
Rajasthan	313
Tamil Nadu	438
Uttar Pradesh	272
West Bengal	291

Source: Indian Labour Journal, Labour Bureau, Ministry of Labour and Employment, 2020

However, the common consensus is that Kerala suffers from a version of 'Dutch disease'.[3] Economists have theorized for long that Kerala's economy and its spending patterns are skewed by the outsized impact of remittances, which shows up as inflation in areas such as wages for unskilled and semi-skilled labour. This is possibly true, as Kerala's manufacturing output is low and the number of

Table 14: Average Daily Wage Rates for Men in Rural India (general agricultural labourers), 2019–20

State	*Average Daily Wage (INR)*
Andhra Pradesh	301
Assam	252
Bihar	257
Gujarat	208
Haryana	392
Himachal Pradesh	418
Karnataka	292
Kerala	701
Madhya Pradesh	198
Maharashtra	231
Odisha	232
Punjab	349
Rajasthan	298
Tamil Nadu	410
Uttar Pradesh	258
West Bengal	267

Source: Indian Labour Journal, Labour Bureau, Ministry of Labour and Employment, 2020

people it employs in manufacturing is also quite low. Yet the wage rates are quite high.

The second highest wages for non-agricultural work, among large states, are found in Tamil Nadu, which doesn't suffer from any version of the Dutch disease. It also has the highest number of factories and workers employed. It's reasonable, therefore, to assume that workers are benefiting from the state's industrialization even if they themselves aren't directly employed in a factory.

Wages for agricultural labour follow a similar pattern, state-wise. The hilly state of Himachal Pradesh, at second position, is sandwiched between Kerala and Tamil Nadu. A quirk in the wage narrative, however, is that average daily wage rates in Maharashtra and Gujarat, two of the most industrialized states, are among the lowest among states.

A day's worth of non-agricultural labour earned a man in rural Gujarat Rs 233 (in 2019–20). In Maharashtra, it earned Rs 240. In Tamil Nadu, a comparable state in terms of industrialization, it earned Rs 438, nearly twice the average wage in Gujarat.

It's possible that because the factories in these western states are relatively advanced and employ fewer people to produce higher outputs, they have no real impact on the wage rates of the masses. It is also possible that some version of semi-skilled labour is in higher demand in the southern states. Perhaps the higher social security net in the southern states results in fairer and better wages for workers. It is also possible that the classification of what's rural is not comparable across these two sets of states (Maharashtra and Gujarat versus Tamil Nadu).

Further, Kerala and Tamil Nadu have had below-replacement fertility rates for a generation, making the labour pool that much smaller. A likely explanation for the wage gap between states is that it's a combination of these afore-mentioned factors and several other factors we haven't even considered.

Whatever the reasons, the fact is the Tamil worker seems to not only have better prospects in terms of finding a job in a factory in his or her state, but also a higher-paying one even outside a factory. The anecdotal evidence, where employers often complain in Tamil Nadu that they aren't able to find workers for low wages, also points to this. From the workers' point of view, the wages probably need to be even higher. It's a virtuous cycle.

A complicating factor is the dismal level of female participation in the labour force in most Indian states. An obvious reason for seeking higher participation of women in the labour force is to improve the overall productivity of society. An even more fundamental reason is personal fulfilment – a person who works to realize her economic potential is likely to live a more fulfilling life. Paid work generates a personal sense of achievement, pride and self-worth.

Greater female employment is also a feature of a more equal society that has higher rates of female literacy and education. Participation of women in the labour force, it appears, is also positively correlated with wages. Himachal Pradesh, with the second highest daily wages among states, has the highest rates of female LFPR as well.

It's a state that has also done quite well in terms of female literacy, along with southern states. Conversely, the state with the country's worst female literacy, Bihar, also has the lowest rates of female LFPR at 4.5 per cent. There's no way for a society to become prosperous if less than 5 in 100 women of working age are actually working.

Fertility Rate: A Tax on Economic Growth

Economic growth and actual prosperity are not always synonymous in the Indian context. Some states have high population growth on top of a high population base. This is particularly true of the states of the Indo-Gangetic plains, which still have above-replacement level fertility rates. Some other states have stable populations. And this affects the way economic growth affects the individual in those states.

Chart 1: Per Capita GSDP (Per Capita NSDP Growth vs NSDP Growth)

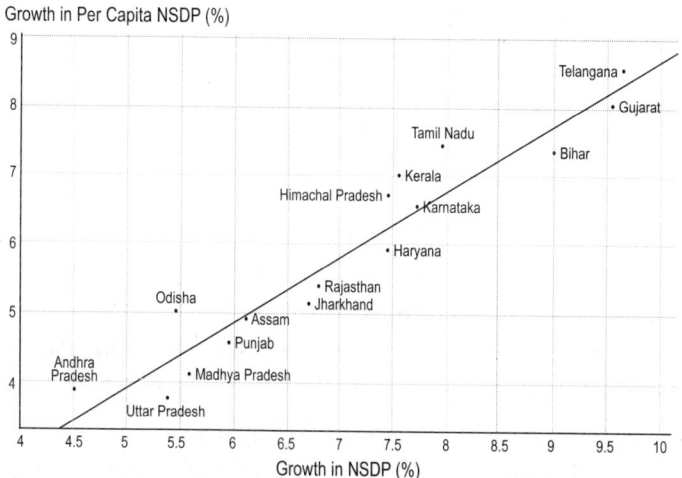

Note: Per capita NSDP for 2018–19, at constant prices. Base year 2011–12
Source: Directorate of Economics and Statistics of respective state governments

The state of Uttar Pradesh, for example, had a NSDP growth of 5.38 per cent in 2018–19 over the previous year. However, for an economy that grew at 5.38 per cent, its per capita NSDP growth was only 3.79 per cent. That is, the state lost almost two percentage points in per capita growth when compared with its own absolute growth (see Chart 1).

In comparison, NSDP growth in Tamil Nadu for the same year was 7.92 per cent while the per capita growth was 7.45 per cent – or, the state mostly realized its growth in per capita terms too.

In other words, Uttar Pradesh pays about two percentage points of its growth as 'tax' towards higher population growth. Whereas all the southern states, by virtue of having had below-replacement fertility rates for over a generation, realize their economic growth almost entirely because their populations have stabilized.

A plotting of per capita NSDP gains against growth of NSDP (Chart 1) reveals that all the southern states, along with Maharashtra and Himachal Pradesh, have a positive residual. That is, their growth in per capita terms is greater for the same level of absolute economic growth, which is not the case with other Indian states. The state that has the highest positive residual, or the state that suffers the least penalty in per capita economic growth because of population growth is Tamil Nadu. It is followed closely in this respect by Kerala, Andhra Pradesh and Telangana.

In effect, the rest of India has to grow faster than south India to achieve the same level of individual prosperity.

This partly explains the finding that different states in India do not converge to a single steady state economically but converge to multiple sets of steady states. Worse, those states with a need to grow faster just to keep pace with those at the forefront are the states that grow slower, simply because their economy is dominated by the majority of people working in agriculture.

The Disaster of GST

India's states, one can reasonably conclude from the data above, are vastly different from one another as economic units. Their growth patterns, their revenue base, their main economic activities, the economic opportunities they provide for their citizens, and their trajectories – all exist in extremely divergent modes.

Consider the large states of the Indo-Gangetic plains – Uttar Pradesh, Madhya Pradesh, Bihar, Rajasthan, Chhattisgarh and Jharkhand. The population of these states put together, at over 500 million, is more than the third most populous country in the world – the USA – by a very large margin. These states, combined, had a total of 39,254 factories in 2017–18. Tamil Nadu, a state with about 70 million people, had 37,787 factories. This is why a single policy for all states is impossible.

In 2017, the Union government introduced a goods and services tax, or GST. It is the most significant nationwide economic policy change in India in the twenty-first century so far. It was sold to the public as the greatest economic reform in independent India – one that would be the answer to India's wicked problems of a poor manufacturing base and a large unemployed population. Inaugurated with much fanfare in a midnight session in Parliament, it has proven to be a bad idea that's been poorly implemented.

The GST is a strange reform to implement, given that the primary concern in India is joblessness among the young. The GST, even when it works well as intended, is likely to negatively impact employment growth in those states that need to create jobs the most. For critics of the idea, the question at the time the GST was being implemented was: why don't the only two federal structures comparable with India in terms of size – China and the USA – have GST or its equivalent?

At its core, the GST aims to shift taxation from the manufacturing centres to the consumption centres and deliver the entire Indian Union as a single market. The idea is that manufacturing something in one state, say, Uttar Pradesh, for tax reasons, is not the most efficient way of manufacturing. To achieve excellence, the reasoning goes, India should concentrate its manufacturing further in states/geographies that have greater efficiencies, such as the manufacturing clusters already present in, say, Maharashtra, rather than at a local facility in Uttar Pradesh. A tax policy that shifts taxation to the point of sale aims to achieve exactly that.

But this begs the question that Uttar Pradesh should now be asking: If we do not have any way to kick-start our manufacturing to meet even local demand, how will we ever build a manufacturing base and expand it so that we can start moving people currently employed in unproductive agriculture into a higher-wage-earning industry like manufacturing? That is a long-term problem for all the states that currently have a low manufacturing base, and GST makes the building of a manufacturing base only harder.

States like Maharashtra, on the other hand, have a different problem: they stand to lose some of their taxing powers and revenue on the goods they manufacture, as taxation is shifted to places of consumption. More importantly, they lose the power of indirect taxation – such as the levying of sales tax – in their own states as part of the agreement to have a uniform tax system nationwide.

For the relatively prosperous states, and the power of indirect taxation is a particularly useful one to have – albeit one that should be used sparingly because it tends to get regressive. In the 1980s, when Chief Minister M.G. Ramachandran announced the expansion of the midday meal scheme in Tamil Nadu to all students in all districts, indirect taxation – specifically sales tax – was one of the avenues the state used to meet the revenue shortfall.

That meal scheme can now take credit for Tamil Nadu's gains, such as female literacy, female LFPR, a college-educated workforce and a strong manufacturing base. The

GST arrangement removes the power of state governments to do such experiments, some of which can yield generational dividends.

More than it being questionable policy in terms of its design, and suboptimal in terms of outcome, the GST is a prime example of India's centralizing impulse, at a time when the needs of its states have diverged beyond any single-policy prescription's ability to manage contradictions. 'One Nation, One Tax' has been a slogan of the Union government apropos the GST. It is catchy and satisfies the business press in the short run. It will probably even help large corporations achieve better scale and greater profits. But the consequences of it in the short term have already been ruinous for state governments.

Under the agreement between the Union and the states, the Union government promised to compensate states if they experienced revenue shortfall for a period of five years. The assumption under which the Union government made this promise was that the GST would result in tax buoyancy – a fancy way of saying the government expected greater revenues from the new tax regime than from the old one. But that did not materialize. In the period between 2017 and 2020, GST buoyancy was lower than that of the taxes it subsumed.

There have been several reasons for the low tax buoyancy. The Fifteenth Finance Commission Report, for example, called the GST non-functional. The Comptroller and Auditor General (CAG) commented on how the most basic idea of GST, of firms receiving input credit for invoices, was not functioning as it should, which resulted in the poor collections.

The Union government also arm-twisted states in the GST Council into cutting rates.[4] These rates have been slashed several times since the original implementation of GST. The Union's rationale is that lower rates incentivize production. The result of those cuts have slashed the effective weighted average of GST from 14.4 per cent to 11.6 per cent. That is a primary reason for the shortfall from the original estimations.

The actions of the Union government betray the perverse incentives of the GST regime for the Union vis-à-vis the states. Cutting rates means states stand to lose their revenue, as over 70 per cent of the total GST collection is supposed to devolve back to the states. A lower total collection affects states directly by impacting their revenues. The GST agreements limit states' options to raise any new revenues to manage this shortfall.

The GST Council, which decides these rate cuts, is constituted as follows: each state has one vote along with the Union, which also has a veto. It's unfair in two ways: the first is that the veto stacks the deck in favour of the Union.

The second is that even when the Union does not use its veto, the very idea of the GST is stacked against manufacturing states. After all, there will be more consuming states than manufacturing states by the very intent of trying to concentrate manufacturing. That would result in the consuming states banding together to seek favourable terms at the expense of the manufacturing states, which are likely to be fewer, historically and by design.

These fears were expressed by the states well before the implementation of the GST regime. The Union sought to assuage the states' fears, saying there would be no revenue shortfall. This was backed by legislation that promised states they'd be compensated for any shortfall if the collections fell below 14 per cent compounded rate from the base year of 2015–16 for a period of five years. This was supposed to be funded by a cess on demerit goods – like tobacco, pan masala, etc., – that the Union government levies. The Union government, in 2020, repeatedly reneged on this promise as the estimated collections did not materialize, either from the GST or the demerit cess.

The Union then asked the states to meet the shortfall in revenue by borrowing that amount from the market. The states, particularly those states to which the Union owes compensation, have all had to struggle with deficits. Unsurprisingly, states like Punjab, Maharashtra, Tamil Nadu and Karnataka have been at the receiving end of this shortfall. With the promised five-year period coming to an end, and given the experience of these five years, it's likely that the GST is going to leave a permanent hole in the budgets of industrialized states.

In the medium and long run, the GST usurps states' rights by rendering state governments incapable of deciding their own tax policies. When state governments cannot choose between sources of revenue to fund policies and projects of their choice, it makes them mere units of policy execution and administration. The GST, in essence, is reducing state governments to glorified bureaucracies.

People elect state governments in the hope of those governments making certain difficult moral choices on their behalf. And many Indian states are much larger than most countries in terms of population.

The choices before Uttar Pradesh, for example, can be these: does it go all out to fix its IMR and school dropout rates by innovating on policies in these areas, or does it carry on like a normal state? It cannot afford to carry on like a normal state, given the high penalty it pays for the poor health and education of its children; but fixing those basic problems is prohibitively expensive as well. The elected state government is supposed to make these very difficult choices on behalf of the voters.

But Tamil Nadu or Maharashtra or Kerala have very different policy needs. Their tax base and possibilities of taxation are a world removed from Uttar Pradesh's; and possibly from each other's too. Those state governments owe their citizens a path to middle-income life. This too will be increasingly difficult under the GST regime.

The Farm Laws

Another important economic policy action in the last decade has been the passing of three laws related to agriculture in

2020, which were together referred to as 'Farm Laws' in the popular press. These would have affected the livelihoods of over half the population and are thus economic policy more than anything else. There were mass protests against these proposed laws. Procedural issues were also raised by the protesters and the press as the laws were rushed through Parliament in the midst of a global pandemic. Beyond these criticisms, the Farm Laws, as they stood, pointed to a disturbing centralization trend.

At their core, these laws made changes in the definition of what constituted farming and what a farm was, how the produce could be stored and traded. Crucially, they dismantled the rights of states to levy certain fees or taxes on trades between the producer and buyer.

On the aspects of changing definitions and terms of trade, experts can differ in good faith. The real constitutional problem with these laws was that they were passed by Parliament on what is a state subject – agriculture. They affect the tax revenue of states and half the people living in those states. As we've seen, there are very wide variances in levels of development among states. It is likely that the policy needed on the terms of trade in Punjab is vastly different from the policy needed in Madhya Pradesh, given that their agricultural yields are so different. Any single given policy laid down by the Union government is unlikely to work for a large number of states.

Yet, that's exactly what these laws set out to do. The protests gathered so much popular support that the Union government relented and repealed these laws. But the protests were over the merits of those laws, not over whether they should be passed by Parliament at all. If the next piece of legislation does not result in such widespread protests, does that give Parliament the right to pass such laws on state subjects? It's a question that time will answer – hopefully, in the negative.

Given the latest report by the Intergovernmental Panel on Climate Change (IPCC) there could be intriguing trajectories for the agricultural sector over the next few decades. Some states could decide that agriculture isn't a worthwhile economic activity since it results in high carbon emissions and environmental degradation.

States whose agricultural contribution to GSDP is low and the proportion of population dependent on agriculture is also low could decide to pay farmers to not sow crops and just let their lands go fallow. They can decide that agriculture is something their state can't afford. Some other states can't think of doing this because of the high proportion of their population dependent on agriculture.

States should ideally have the freedom to decide their agricultural policies, even if they decide to take such radical steps. It is both their political right and what's good for the planet. However, the farm laws that were passed wouldn't have allowed that to happen in any meaningful way, given that the terms of trade are centrally defined. What's worse is that the Union government runs a nationwide programme called PM KISAN, which in effect pays farmers to continue farming. It's a cash assistance scheme for those farmers who own land and can prove it using title deeds.

It's probably a reasonable short-term thing for a government to do in some states, given the crisis in agriculture. But in some other states, where there are enough non-farm opportunities and where farm yields are close to global averages, it's probably unnecessary and even counterproductive. Further, landownership patterns and implementation of land reforms are uneven across states; which is why a centralized cash assistance programme based on landownership is again going to be unfair to the landless agricultural workers. Any such centralized scheme in India, however well intentioned, is doomed to failure, given the country's size and population.

Many of India's state governments, constrained by the Union in what they can and can't do in several areas that relate to the economy, seem to have decided to woo foreign direct investment in the last couple of decades as the route to success in the economic realm. Several state governments make splashy advertisements of investor summits that result in investment agreements that don't often fructify. These states, because they compete amongst themselves, offer large tax and land concessions to multinational companies. These favourable terms often don't make economic sense to the states. Yet they are locked in a battle to attract maximum investments and prestige projects, and one can't fault them for it.

The basic truth that state governments, and any

government for that matter, can improve the economic prospects of its citizens by ensuring a healthy, well-educated population that's capable of holding productive jobs is lost in the race to attract big business. Companies seek to invest in places where there's skilled labour available at competitive wages, and where the rule of law is upheld. These are basic governance issues that do not need fancy investor summits; but they do need governments to carry out the hard work of building schools, of keeping children in school, of ensuring that enough of them go to college, and above all, to wait patiently for a generation for all this to show results.

Other factors for success are a robust and compassionate criminal justice system and a 'high-trust' society. At least, that's what the experience from multiple countries suggests. A relative social safety net with high degrees of female literacy and educational achievement are additional factors for any place to become a modern-day hub of economic activity.

That takes hard but unglamorous work, which also demands a lot of room for policy experimentation and yields results on a generational time scale. The Indian Union, though, seems to be working towards the exact opposite goal, reducing the space for policy experimentation amongst states, centralizing as much decision-making as possible and legislating with procedural lapses, making them more vulnerable to repeal.

4

Why Has the South Performed Better?

State of the States

The data for India's states across the sectors of health, economy and education raises two obvious questions: why has peninsular India done better and how can the divergences between the states ever be addressed in policymaking?

Subnationalism is a frequently cited reason. A greater focus on education in the southern states is attributed to political movements that emphasized self-respect, which in turn resulted in better development for them. Some of these movements were also explicitly anti-caste, which has been attributed to consolidation of the subaltern, yielding a sense of solidarity and common purpose.

Others have attributed the improvements narrowly to specific policies, such as midday meals which helped keep children in school, regardless of whether those were the result of such subnational consolidation. Still others have cited cultural and anthropological reasons and practices, such as marriage among cousins – where a woman who marries into her extended family has slightly more agency than a woman married into a home outside the family network. Economists also like to cite better access to the sea.

The answer is probably all the above, and then some.

Motivated reasoning, confirmation bias and a genuine inability to distinguish cause from effect make pinpointing the reasons why southern states have done better than their northern counterparts a difficult question to answer.

A crucial aspect of the divergence is that India's best states were not always the best. Their improvement and outcomes can be explained by policy actions and the politics that enabled those over the last few generations. Present-day Kerala, which is a consistent leader in most development indicators across health and education, for example, was considered a basket case in the late nineteenth century. The situation was so bad that the British were constantly threatening to annex what was then the princely state of Travancore and merge it with the Madras Presidency.

The states of Travancore, Cochin, and what is present-day northern Kerala did not see themselves as a single society. Travancore's caste system was rigid even by the standards of the nineteenth century, and the majority of the population lived in conditions that the British administrators thought were cruel. Travancore's elite Brahmins were not originally from the state, causing further complications and disaffection among the people. There was no concept of a 'Malayalee'; back then, that term generally meant someone belonging to the Nair caste. In effect, Travancore was a state without a cohesive identity and its people lived in abject poverty with no health or education to speak of.

By the late nineteenth and early twentieth centuries, a fledgling movement called the Aikya Kerala movement started to protest the dominance of Brahmins in the region. What started as a demand for representation in jobs soon morphed into a movement that went well beyond its original cause. It forged an identity for the Malayalee people for the first time.

The real effect of the movement, historians agree, was that it made society seek public services for the entire society as Malayalee people, as opposed to seeking favours for particular caste groups. This transformed the health and education services in ways that we still see evidence of. The transformation wasn't overnight, or easy. But the slow struggle to transform society ended in success, partly because the citizens thought of themselves as one linguistic unit.

Neighbouring Tamil Nadu had the non-Brahmin movement, which started a few decades after the Aikya Kerala movement. Later, this morphed into the Justice Party and continues to this day in the form of the offshoots of the Dravidian movement. Much like the Aikya Kerala movement, the Dravidian movement started as a protest for better representation of the people in jobs before becoming a subnationalist movement about Tamil causes and identity, seeking to unify Tamilians against Brahmins first, and later against New Delhi and Hindi imposition.

The effect of the Dravidian movement, much like that of the Aikya Kerala movement, was one of consolidating the Tamil identity. Public services are now seen as public services for the Tamil people, as a whole. This, again, is credited in literature as one of the driving forces behind improvements in health and education in the state.

Andhra Pradesh, Telangana and Karnataka have also shown a higher degree of subnationalism than the rest of India. Their welfare policies – particularly in areas of supplemental nutrition, health and education – distinctly belong to southern India. Andhra Pradesh and Telangana have generous public distribution systems, for example. In the context of the budgetary constraints that India's states face, the southern states, in general, privilege universal access over targeting, unlike the states in the Indo-Gangetic plains, or the recommendations of the Union government.

A renewed sense of localized kinship amongst an old 'in-group' of a given society – which may be ethnic, or linguistic, or any other such axis of identification – has proven to be a common thread amongst societies that made rapid advances in the nineteenth and twentieth centuries. Finland and Japan are frequently cited examples of this.

A feeling of 'my society' among people with respect to their 'in-group' seems to make them view public goods such as health and education as something beyond a zero-sum game between competing communities or subgroups. India, with a population of 1.3 billion and multiple internal cleavages, makes that feeling of a strong 'in-group' near impossible to achieve for the entire country. What the right size of a group is for such a feeling to be fostered is a difficult question to answer; but if the rest of the world is any guide, it isn't anywhere near the population of India.

The sense of subnationalism and of common identity is difficult to forge. But once forged, it's a great force multiplier, as the experience in southern India has shown. People will have to have a sense of belonging for public services to be effective. It's in this context that people also feel a positive connection with their society, when their tax money is spent for the development of that society. It strengthens their bond with society and creates a virtuous cycle. And locally designed welfare programmes tailored to a society's needs give its people a sense of participation, improving that sense of belonging even further.

Why Does the Indian Union Exist in Its Current Form?

The answer depends on whom we ask this question of. Hindu nationalists may attribute the raison d'être for India's existence as a modern republic to their view of India being a civilizational state based on religion. Secular liberals may attribute it to the freedom movement, the anti-colonial struggle and the constitutional values that stemmed from them. Most people (who probably aren't either) will likely think that India exists in its current shape because of a combination of those and a hundred other factors. In other words, India exists for the same reason any country exists in the modern world – it's a historical accident.

In India's case, given its enormous population, disparity and diversity, it's a miracle of an accident. And it is even more miraculous that it has sustained for seventy-five years in its current form of being an electoral democracy that conducts periodic elections that are generally free and largely fair. For a country of its scale and complexity – especially one that was born out of an anti-colonial struggle – this is unheard of elsewhere in the world.

The positive connotations of the word 'miracle' often preclude questions on whether the intended liberal democracy works the way it's expected to. This comes down to whether the various subgroups and regions are happy with their place and influence in India. A country that's as large as ours, merely by virtue of the power it generates out of its being large, often has the ability to sustain internal contradictions for some time. This can take the form of benign status quo bias, or a less benign illiberal, majoritarian rule.

The different segments in India could possibly think of the 'miracle' differently, therefore. The Hindi-speaking Hindu majority of the Indo-Gangetic plains that forms the largest ethno-linguistic-religious group in the country possibly looks at India as a mirror of itself, if the politics of the twenty-first century is any guide. The many other ethno-linguistic groups that have a long history pre-dating the modern republic likely see themselves and India in distinctly different ways.

Whatever the reasons India exists in its current form, governance is a colossal challenge in this union of vastly divergent states. It's also clear, again from their very divergence, that whatever central policy anyone comes up with cannot serve all of the states, or even a handful of them, well.

It's impossible for a single policy solution to work for both the best and worst performing states of India. The states of central and northern India need to focus on input metrics to deal with their policy problems in health and education, while the states of southern India have to look at output metrics, given their growth stage. And each state needs its own unique tweaks within those broad buckets too. Karnataka, for instance, has its own quirks, despite being in the southern bucket. As do Haryana and Punjab in their respective buckets.

Does the Indian Union Work?

A simple test of whether a democracy is functional is this: Does it allow a self-governing people to proceed on a slow march towards enlightened liberalism? India's answer to that was never an enthusiastic yes. In the time since Independence, that march towards liberalism has taken several dark detours that even the loudest nationalist won't deny.

Examining utilitarian outcomes of governance in each state, in the areas of health, education and economic opportunities, is a useful place to start. Whether the political Union allows India's states the policy space to meet and accommodate the aspirations of their citizens is another crucial question in assessing the health of India's overall democracy. Whatever a given state's achievements, or lack thereof, the system should allow all its citizens to feel they have the right to self-determination, which will allow them to work towards the light at the end of the tunnel.

What India needs is a political structure that allows for states – and other subunits of society – to organize themselves, devise their own policies, and have sufficient resources to fund those policies. More importantly, in doing so, the country must retain the democratic sanctity of the process by which the subunits arrive at those policy decisions. After all, that is the only way to maximize developmental outcomes while minimizing possible conflicts.

Arriving at the right policy is quite often an accident. Sustaining and improving that policy is what needs concerted action, knowledge and sacrifice. The ability to arrive at that policy option, or more importantly, the ability to choose from multiple iterations of a policy to arrive at what works, is why the structure of decision-making is far more important than any single decision itself. The purpose of such a structure, above all, should be one that makes people feel empowered. What is the political structure that will allow India's states or regions or subunits to achieve this? The next parts of the book will explore this.

Part II
India's Wicked Problems

Introduction: Is South India an Equal Partner?

India, as the first sentence of the Constitution reminds us, is a Union of states. The unit of consideration for resource allocation, power sharing and realpolitik in the country is the state. Achieving relative equilibria amongst states in these various aspects, through democratic means, is a necessary condition for a stable Union.

In the last half century though, that compact between states has been eroding. The southern states have a difficult bargain on their hands. They face the threat of losing their political power and relevance with impending delimitation, which may drastically reduce their representation in Parliament. They are already losing out massively on their share of tax revenues; they receive far less than they contribute to the exchequer owing to their populations having stabilized. That is, they are likely to lose political power and at the same time be subject to unjust taxation, which requires political power to fight against in the first place.

The space for policymaking that will suit the circumstances of the southern states is set to shrink, as a result. Their cultural and linguistic anxieties will also peak, as the northern plains impose their demographic might on the Indian Union. This comes at a time when the divergence in the development trajectories of India's states calls for greater space for them in both policymaking and budgetary freedom. The bind that southern India finds itself in is unique; it's unlike any situation in most large federal unions across the world.

This part of the book explores demographic divergence and fiscal federalism in India, two of the most important manifestations of the country's deteriorating compact.

1

Population Divergence

India's ability to provide basic health services, to build schools, to keep children in school, to achieve prosperity and to meet every other challenge to basic governance is complicated in the extreme as a result of its huge population and its continuing high rate of population growth. Demographic reality cannot be circumvented – people show up.

Population isn't merely a rate-limiting step for policymaking in a technical sense. More people don't merely demand bigger infrastructure and more services, they also happen to be the fuel for democracy. They bend governments and policy towards themselves.

Population growth in any one segment with respect to another results in shifts in political power. This is particularly fraught with problems in a diverse federal union like India, which already has a large population that is still growing exponentially and in an extremely divergent manner across states. This skew of demographic and political might towards one part of India, and away from another, in some senses, is India's biggest problem.

Population Growth = Poverty

The most commonly quoted and critiqued ideas on population growth in a society and its relationship to the economy came over 200 years ago from the pen of Thomas Robert Malthus, the English cleric and polymath.

In his work published in 1798, called 'An Essay on the Principle of Population', Malthus argued that population grows exponentially while food production grows linearly. This meant that even if a society achieved relative abundance, it would soon end up with a population growth that strained the available resources. The Malthusian Trap describes a situation where any improvement in availability of resources and abundance is a temporary phenomenon; once the population catches up, the society's per capita indicators return to their original lower levels.

The assumptions and conclusions of Malthus have since been criticized by many from many different points of view. Karl Marx, a few generations later, criticized Malthus for what we'd now call scientism.

Marx disagreed with the premise that overpopulation could be explained away by laws of nature and argued that capitalist means of production had an even greater role in explaining abundance, or its lack thereof. The assumption that we'd be able to produce near-infinite resources for sustaining life for an exponentially growing population lies at one end of the spectrum; Marx, while not suggesting that explicitly, was somewhat in that camp. The assumption that production capacity is static lies at the other end of the spectrum, which is where Malthus has been unfairly placed for much of the last two centuries.

The truth, as we now realize, is somewhere along that scale. But here's the non-trivial question: Is population growth impeding the quality of life that would otherwise have been possible?

Marx's collaborator Engels seemed to agree with Malthus. Malthus himself, even in his own time, was in continual debate with the philosopher William Goodwin, today more famously known as the father of the author of *Frankenstein*, Mary Shelley. In 1820, some two decades after 'An Essay on the Principle of Population' was published, Goodwin wrote a formal rebuttal to Malthus, offering an argument we may recognize: he disputed Malthus's central assertion, which was that population would double every twenty-five years.

Goodwin argued that Malthus's assumed fertility rate was too high. Malthus had assumed it to be eight children per woman. This was during a time before census data was easily available for statistical analysis, and before even statistical analysis was a commonly used tool. Goodwin's argument does seem ironic in another way, since he himself was one of thirteen children.

However, Malthus's ideas remain influential today because he postulated two important things: the TFR is what determines population growth; and exponential population growth does put pressure on available resources, particularly in a society that isn't industrially developed.

The most basic predictor of population growth, we now know, is indeed the TFR. That is, the population of the future is obviously determined by how many children each woman has over her lifetime, on average. A TFR of 2.1 is now considered 'replacement level', one that would achieve a stable population. A TFR less than 2.1 points to a declining population in the future if the trend continues; and a higher TFR value points to growth in population.

India and the Malthusian Trap

Post-Independence India in the mid-twentieth century was a textbook case for Malthus's prediction. Population growth was outpacing the country's ability to feed itself in the early years after Independence. Foodgrains made available through foreign aid sustained the country for a while. The government had to respond to this crisis, and it did so in complicated and illiberal ways, which did not cover India in glory. Neither did those measures fully achieve the intended results, given that India still had a TFR above-replacement levels as late as in 2020.

India adopted a two-pronged strategy to deal with the Malthusian Trap in the 1970s. One was to control population growth in order to curtail demand, while the other was to implement modern farming techniques to improve yields. The improvements in agriculture, thanks to the green revolution, have alleviated food scarcity to a large extent. Yields in India are still poor compared with global averages, as seen in the previous chapters. But at least they are sufficient to feed the population now, and have been sufficient for a generation now.

The other part of this strategy – controlling population growth – has yielded even more uneven results. Some states have done quite well, while others still have TFRs that are predictive of exponential population growth. There was an aggressive campaign to reduce family size; incentive programmes for voluntary sterilization were launched and there were even reports of forced sterilization during India's Emergency in 1975–77.

Interestingly, during the Cold War years, there was also American pressure to limit population growth as part of their fight against communism. The prevailing theory was that population growth in poor countries resulted in communist revolutions; or at the least a high growth in population, combined with existing poverty, the dogma went, made populations susceptible to communism. This meant American pressure on governments across South Asia goading nations to act to control population growth. This was a significant factor.

Given the convergence of motivations, incentives and circumstances, population control did become national policy in the mid-1970s. The primary responsibility of implementing this national policy of population control, however, fell on state governments. Health and education, the two levers any government has to implement population control, happened to be state subjects. And the most potent tool for population control, it turned out, wasn't a forced sterilization drive or government campaigns that asked people to have fewer children. Instead, it consisted of sending girls to school.

This policy, as is the case with every other policy, was uneven in terms of its implementation across India's states. Malthus claimed populations would double, given the conditions of the late eighteenth century. Even in his time his critics thought that was too high a rate. But in India, that prediction was terrifyingly accurate for some states in the late twentieth century (see Table 1)!

Table 1: Growth in Population from 1971 to 2011

State	*Population Growth (%)*
Rajasthan	166
Haryana	157
Bihar	146
Madhya Pradesh	142
Uttar Pradesh	138
Jharkhand	132
Gujarat	126
Uttarakhand	125
Maharashtra	123
Chhattisgarh	119
Assam	113

State	Population Growth (%)
Karnataka	109
West Bengal	106
Punjab	104
Himachal Pradesh	98
Odisha	91
Goa	83
Tamil Nadu	75
Kerala	56

Source: Census 1971 and Census 2011, Office of the Registrar General and Census Commissioner, Ministry of Home Affairs

Rajasthan, for example, had a population of 25.7 million in 1971. In 2011 its population was 68.6 million. Rajasthan's population grew by 166 per cent in forty years, more than doubling in twenty-five years, even faster than Malthus's prediction. Bihar, Madhya Pradesh and Uttar Pradesh were all just short of doubling their respective populations, growing at near Malthus's predicted rate during the same period.

While the states of the Indo-Gangetic plains experienced growth rates that saw the doubling of their populations every twenty-five years as late as during the late twentieth century – even after population control was declared a policy of national importance – peninsular India charted a different trajectory. Kerala's population grew by only 56 per cent in those forty years, at roughly a third of the rate Malthus had predicted.

In other words, from one perspective, Rajasthan is Malthus's nightmare, while Kerala is Goodwin's dream. The two states had comparable populations in 1971. But in 2011, Rajasthan had more than twice the number of people as Kerala. They are no longer comparable states.

India's Demographic Divergence

Many states in India have now stabilized their TFRs and have achieved below-replacement values. The states of West Bengal, Tamil Nadu, Andhra Pradesh, Punjab and Himachal Pradesh, for example, all had TFRs of 1.6 in 2017 (see Table 2). That's lower than China's TFR of 1.7, which was achieved in that country only after a generation of forced one-child policy.

Table 2: TFR by State and UTs

State	TFR
Andhra Pradesh	1.6
Assam	2.3
Bihar	3.2
Chhattisgarh	2.4
Gujarat	2.2
Haryana	2.2
Himachal Pradesh	1.6
Jammu and Kashmir	1.6
Jharkhand	2.5
Karnataka	1.7

State	TFR
Kerala	1.7
Madhya Pradesh	2.7
Maharashtra	1.7
Odisha	1.9
Punjab	1.6
Rajasthan	2.6
Tamil Nadu	1.6
Telangana	1.7
Uttar Pradesh	3.0
West Bengal	1.6

Note: TFR by residence for India and bigger states/UTs for 2017
Source: Census 2018, Census Division, Office of the Registrar General and Census Commissioner, Ministry of Home Affairs

On the contrary, states like Uttar Pradesh, Bihar, Madhya Pradesh, Rajasthan, Jharkhand, Chhattisgarh, et al., have higher-than-replacement TFRs still, some half a century after the adoption of population control as national policy. Bihar's TFR, for example, was 3.2 in 2017. It's no wonder, therefore, that the states which grew the fastest in terms of population in the last fifty years are the states that still have above-replacement TFRs.

For a society that had above-replacement TFRs for a long time, a dip in TFRs to below-replacement levels takes a few generations to reflect as an absolute decline in population. After all, a lot of children were already born when the TFRs were high in the recent past. They will have fewer children in turn. But this will still result in population growth, as long as they and their children are still alive. In contrast, an above-replacement TFR has an immediate exponential effect on population growth.

Table 3: Population Under 15 Years of Age and TFR

State	Population Under 15 Years of Age (%)	TFR (2016)
Bihar	43.8	3.3
Uttar Pradesh	42.3	3.1
Jharkhand	39.5	2.6
Rajasthan	38.9	2.7
Madhya Pradesh	37.3	2.8
Chhattisgarh	35.6	2.5
Assam	34.9	2.3
Haryana	34.7	2.3
Odisha	32.1	2.0
Jammu and Kashmir	32.0	1.7
West Bengal	31.9	1.6
Gujarat	31.6	2.2
Karnataka	30.9	1.8
Maharashtra	30.6	1.8
Punjab	29.6	1.7
Himachal Pradesh	29.3	1.7
Tamil Nadu	26.6	1.6
Kerala	25.4	1.8

Sources: NITI Aayog and NFHS-4

For example, Kerala has only 25.4 per cent of its population under 15 years of age – the lowest among all states (see Table 3). This is the effect of its long-term TFR being below replacement level. Its current TFR will also act on this subset of girls under the age of 15, who will become mothers in the next two decades. And on top of this, Kerala has below-replacement TFR, which means these children's children will be fewer than their own population cohort. Given a lower number of children to begin with, who will be tomorrow's parents and who will have fewer children too, the overall population gradually reduces.

On the contrary, Bihar has 44 per cent of its population under the age of fifteen. And it has a TFR of 3.2. That is, these children of today – who are already a large proportion of the population – will go on to have an even larger number of children than their own cohort numbers.

These cascading effects of current base and future TFRs were what Malthus was worried about. These effects explain the divergence in population growth estimates for Indian states in the next decades. Tamil Nadu, for instance, is expected to experience an annual decline in population growth for the decade 2031–41. Andhra Pradesh is estimated to be near stable. But Bihar will still have an annual growth of 1 per cent in its population for the next decade (see Table 4).

Table 4: Estimate of Annual Population Growth Rate for Major States for 2031–41

State	Annual Population Growth (%)
Tamil Nadu	-0.1
Andhra Pradesh	0.0
Karnataka	0.1
Punjab	0.1
West Bengal	0.1
Maharashtra	0.2
Kerala	0.2
Himachal Pradesh	0.2
Delhi	0.3
Odisha	0.4
Gujarat	0.4
Haryana	0.4
Assam	0.5
Jammu and Kashmir	0.5
Chhattisgarh	0.6
Madhya Pradesh	0.6
Uttar Pradesh	0.7
Rajasthan	0.8
Jharkhand	0.8
Bihar	1.0

Sources: Census 2011, IIPS and *Economic Survey 2018–19*, Vol. 1, Department of Economic Affairs, Ministry of Finance, July 2019

It's a relatively well-understood phenomenon that population growth metrics, particularly TFR, best respond to female literacy and education. Across societies and ethnicities, and among communities of various religious backgrounds too, the more educated women are the fewer children they have.

Iran, an Islamic theocracy, has managed to drop its TFR from 6.52 in 1981 to below-replacement levels in the present day, for example.[1] Iran happens to also have a greater number of women attending college than men. This link did not escape the attention of its ruling theocracy, which sought to limit women's access to college. Vietnam, a communist country, has also managed to drop its TFR on the back of improved education levels among its women.[2] Sri Lanka[3] and Thailand,[4] countries with Buddhist majorities, have also now achieved below-replacement TFRs.

Among India's states, unsurprisingly again, TFR tends to be higher where female illiteracy is higher (see Table 5). Bihar, Jharkhand, Rajasthan, Madhya Pradesh and Uttar Pradesh have the most illiterate women in the reproductive age as a proportion of their population. These are also states in India whose TFRs are still above replacement levels.

Table 5: Illiterate Female Population in the Age Group 15–49, 2017

State	Illiterate Female Population (%)
Andhra Pradesh	15.5
Assam	11.3
Bihar	26.8
Chhattisgarh	17.1

State	Illiterate Female Population (%)
Gujarat	17.2
Haryana	12.3
Himachal Pradesh	1.2
Jammu and Kashmir	16.9
Jharkhand	24.9
Karnataka	6.1
Kerala	0.7
Madhya Pradesh	19.2
Maharashtra	4.5
Odisha	11.8
Punjab	9.4
Rajasthan	22.5
Tamil Nadu	3.8
Telangana	17.5
Uttar Pradesh	22.4
West Bengal	11.2

Source: Census of India, Census Division, Office of the Registrar General and Census Commissioner, Ministry of Home Affairs

More than just with rising basic literacy, TFR tends to reduce if there's a greater level of education among women (see Table 6). That is, women who are college educated have fewer children than those with just a high school education; these high school-educated women in turn have fewer children than those who dropped out earlier from school. The trick, then, to achieve the intended goal of population control is to have a lot more women with a college education, and very few who don't, among those of reproductive age;

and to maximize the number of years in school for women who are not inclined to go to college.

Table 6: TFR by Level of Education of Women in States/UTs, 2017

State	Below Primary	Primary	Middle	Class X	Class XII	Graduate and Above
Andhra Pradesh	2.0	2.1	2.1	1.9	1.5	1.1
Assam	2.6	2.8	2.3	2.3	2.1	2.0
Bihar	4.3	3.5	3.3	2.8	2.5	1.9
Chhattisgarh	3.5	2.8	2.8	2.5	2.0	1.8
Gujarat	3.7	2.7	2.6	2.0	1.6	1.3
Haryana	2.6	2.8	2.5	2.5	2.1	1.6
Himachal Pradesh	2.5	2.0	2.1	2.0	1.6	1.5
Jammu and Kashmir	4.5	3.1	2.6	1.4	1.1	0.8
Jharkhand	5.9	4.3	2.6	1.5	1.2	0.2
Karnataka	2.6	2.4	2.2	1.7	1.5	1.0
Kerala	0.6	1.2	2.2	1.8	1.8	1.8
Madhya Pradesh	3.9	3.3	2.9	2.3	2.1	1.8
Maharashtra	1.8	2.2	2.2	2.0	1.5	1.2
Odisha	2.4	2.2	2.1	1.8	1.7	1.2
Punjab	2.1	2.0	1.7	1.9	1.5	1.3
Rajasthan	6.8	2.9	1.6	1.7	2.5	0.6
Tamil Nadu	2.1	2.1	2.3	2.0	1.7	1.1
Telangana	2.1	2.3	2.1	1.9	1.8	1.5

State	Below Primary	Primary	Middle	Class X	Class XII	Graduate and Above
Uttar Pradesh	3.6	3.5	3.1	2.9	2.6	2.4
West Bengal	2.0	2.0	1.7	1.4	1.3	1.1

Source: Census of India, Census Division, Office of the Registrar General and Census Commissioner, Ministry of Home Affairs

As the data on school dropout rates and GER from the chapter on Education suggests, peninsular India manages to retain the most children – of either gender – in school for the longest periods. The southern states also have higher GERs in tertiary education. All of this points to more women having a greater number of years of education in these states. It's not a surprise, then, that these states also have the lowest population growth, with at least one of them set to experience negative growth in the next decade.

The Problem of Delimitation

The data on population growth, or the divergence in that growth across states in the last half century, tells a story of the Indian Union's intractable problem. The states in the Indo-Gangetic plains, with notable exceptions like Punjab and West Bengal, have, over the forty-year period between 1971 and 2011, proved Malthus right.

States in peninsular India, meanwhile, have converged with Western societies and have had population growths that are, at times, half their northern counterparts. In a democracy, we allocate power and resources on the basis of population. We also make decisions that govern people based on that allocated power. All of this follows from and complements the basic maxim of 'one person, one vote'. The population control policy and its uneven implementation may destroy that compact.

The year 1976 was not a great one for liberal democracy in India. After the Emergency was declared in June 1975, the Indira Gandhi-led government had suspended civil liberties and cancelled elections. Political opponents were jailed and courts rendered powerless. The Forty-second Amendment to India's Constitution enacted in that period is perhaps the most illiberal change made to India's Constitution.

It sought to concentrate powers in the hands of the prime minister and dismantled the system of checks and balances by curtailing the powers of judicial review. Yet, there's one tiny part of that very amendment – illiberal and totalitarian as it may be – that has arguably managed the growing contradictions between the states and held the Union together in the last half century.

The original provision of the Indian Constitution, as in most other liberal democracies, was for seat allocation in Parliament to be apportioned based on population, as reflected in the most recent decennial census data. This exercise is foundational to the idea of a legitimate democracy. After all, we want the will of the people to be reflected in a democracy. And the way to ensure that is to make sure all voters are equally represented in Parliament. This is enabled by a periodic delimitation exercise, which recommends the number of seats each state will be given, according to its population.

The Forty-second Amendment froze the delimitation exercise because of the population control drive that the government had undertaken. The thinking went as follows: if one state implemented the population control policy well and another didn't, we'd end up with a situation where the state that implemented it well would have fewer people in the future than the one that did not. This is exactly what has happened with Kerala and Rajasthan, for example. The reason delimitation was frozen was to not reward a Rajasthan with more Members of Parliaments (MPs) for its failure and punish a Kerala with fewer MPs for its success.

The Forty-second Amendment froze the delimitation exercise for a period of twenty-five years. This was subsequently extended to another twenty-five years in 2001. That freeze lasts until 2026. The question is, what happens after that? If the freeze is allowed to expire, it will mean punishing the southern states that have had the most success in population control. If the freeze is extended, it will mean reducing the voice of the people in the Indo-Gangetic plains further, thus rendering the democratic compact unequal.

Tamil Nadu is the state that made the greatest gains in representation owing to the freeze and a slowing down of its population growth. If the delimitation exercise had not been frozen, Tamil Nadu would have seven fewer MPs than it currently has, owing to the divergence of population size among states. In other words, Tamil Nadu currently has seven more MPs in the Lok Sabha than it would have had if the Forty-second Amendment had not been passed.

At the other end of the spectrum, Uttar Pradesh is represented by nine fewer MPs in the Lok Sabha currently than would have been its strength had each decennial census resulted in the reapportioning of parliamentary seats among states.

Kerala and Andhra Pradesh (inclusive of Telangana) are the other two states, apart from Tamil Nadu, which stand to lose the most if the freeze is allowed to lapse. Bihar, Rajasthan and Madhya Pradesh are the other states, apart from Uttar Pradesh, that would gain seats commensurate with the losses of their southern counterparts if the freeze were lifted.

Consider Uttar Pradesh. The state's population, according to the 2011 census was 203 million. It has eighty MPs representing those 203 million people in the Lok Sabha. That is, each MP represents over 2.5 million people. In the case of Tamil Nadu, its thirty-nine MPs represent 72 million people; that is, each of its MPs represents 1.8 million people. Basic arithmetic shows that the average Tamil citizen had about 30 per cent more representation in the Lok Sabha than her counterpart in Uttar Pradesh in 2011.

This divergence in power, much like the population itself, will only grow exponentially. NFHS-5 data pegs the ratios of children under fifteen years of age at 31 per cent of the population for Uttar Pradesh and 21 per cent for

Tamil Nadu. That is, there's a 10 percentage point difference between the two states in the ratio of children under fifteen that make up their respective populations. And this 10 percentage point difference exists on a much higher base population for Uttar Pradesh.

A rough back-of-the-envelope calculation suggests that between 2011 and 2026, Uttar Pradesh will have added over 62 million adult citizens as voters. This would mean a single MP for 3.36 million people in the current scenario. In the same time period, Tamil Nadu would have added a corresponding 15 million, which would mean 2.2 million people per MP. That is, the value of each vote and the representative power of each citizen is diverging to a point where 'one person, one vote' will no longer be true for these two states if the status quo of frozen delimitation persists.

Rajasthan, Bihar, Madhya Pradesh, Chhattisgarh and Jharkhand too have rapidly eroding representation in Parliament per citizen. The opposite is true for the southern states. Every citizen in the southern state has a greater representation in Parliament now than earlier, simply because their states have had a slower population growth and delimitation had been frozen for five decades.

Impact of a Single Vote

The southern states now have a higher representational ratio for their citizens than their northern counterparts, in terms of the total number of MPs they send to Parliament relative to their population. This is a hard-won privilege, given that it has come at the cost of significant social change.

While the overall power of representation has dramatically weakened at the state level across the Indo-Gangetic plains, the population pressures at the constituency level weaken the impact of each vote there. Let's consider the median constituency in terms of number of voters in the two states we considered earlier – Tamil Nadu and Uttar Pradesh. Tenkasi, with 1.492 million electors, and Azamgarh, with 1.789 million electors, are the median constituencies in those two states in terms of size of the electorate.

Let us consider the probability of the individual vote deciding the elections in Tenkasi. This we can call the vote's impact. For ease of calculation, let's assume it's a bipolar race – say, between DMK and the All India Anna Dravida Munnetra Kazhagam (AIDMK). One way to estimate this probability is to assume an odd number of total voters, 'N'. Further, let's assume that N-1 votes have been cast and counted so far, and we have a tie. So the last vote, which is the one we are interested in, is going to break that tie and decide the elections. Let's assume that the probability of a voter choosing DMK is 'p', and of choosing AIADMK 'q'. These two numbers p,q, are obviously very close to each other, and also both very close to 0.5 (or half).

If p and q are not exactly 0.5, which they cannot be, since one party will receive one vote more in our thought experiment, the total number of votes the DMK receives must differ from its expectation of N/2 by $|p-0.5|N$ (the absolute value of the difference between p and 0.5 as a ratio of the total electorate).

This situation is commonly modelled as one of binomial distribution, and while the probability of our one 'golden vote' impacting the ultimate result is absurdly low, we can calculate this to be approximately 1/1221 for Tenkasi, a constituency of 1.492 million, since it will be the inverse of the square root of the total number of voters ($1/\sqrt{1.492}$ million). For Azamgarh, with a voting population of 1.789 million, the probability of impact of a single vote is 1/1337.

That is, in a very close race, the Tamil Nadu voter in a mid-sized constituency has about 10 per cent greater impact in an election than her fellow citizen in Uttar Pradesh, simply because of the total number of voters in those constituencies. This is over and above the overall representation for the two states being divergent. The Tamil Nadu voter has a greater say in electing her MP, and her state has more MPs representing fewer people.

It's important to understand that the starting point for these two states, however, in both state-level representation ratio and constituency-wise probability of impact of a single vote, was the same before the Forty-second Amendment was enacted.

It's since the freezing of the delimitation exercise that the divergence has widened so significantly. In other words, we had a race with the same starting point and well-defined rules. We now have two sets of runners: those running ahead and those running far behind. To ask those running ahead to stop while the others catch up would be unfair; and asking those running so far behind to continue running in the same race would make the race pointless.

Short of making these separate races, this would be an intractable problem to solve. If the delimitation freeze is allowed to expire, it will mean punishing the southern states for their success in implementing a policy decision. If the freeze continues, the compact of 'one person, one vote' does not hold for the country as a whole.

A solution that's frequently suggested to solve this problem is to add more seats in Parliament and skew the ratio of newly added seats to those states where the population growth has been higher.

But in mathematical terms, and politically too, that solution is hardly different from the standard delimitation, which takes seats away from some states and gives them to some others while maintaining the overall count of seats in Parliament. Power sharing is a zero-sum game. No window dressing will alter that equation.

Having a lot of new MPs added to Uttar Pradesh for example, will improve the representation per citizen in that state and improve that citizen's ability to impact the election in her constituency. And this would come at the cost of diminishing a citizen's power and representation in states like Tamil Nadu, Kerala and Andhra Pradesh.

The basic problem with India's electoral democracy, therefore, is: southern states implemented population control and therefore enjoy greater per capita parliamentary representation for their people. And people in the northern states will look at that greater representation and cry foul, saying it's not true democracy if all citizens don't have equal representation in Parliament. Either the southern states have to give up power as a punishment for having effectively implemented a policy of the Union, or the people in the northern Indian states have to accept their status as lesser citizens in terms of political power.

Perhaps the only real solution, short of disbanding the entire system, in such a situation, is to limit the desirability or importance of power sharing between the stakeholders of the system. That is, change the division of powers between the Centre and the states by reducing the powers allocated to the Centre.

That solution points to extreme decentralization and a more equitable federal structure and, perhaps, far more devolution of powers down to the panchayat, municipal and even individual levels.

After all, a basic feature of many things in India – from policy to population growth – has been divergence. When an extremely divergent system is unable to fairly determine a single axis through which all decisions are made, it's only fair to make that axis decide as little as possible while still retaining it.

A possible route towards such a solution is proposed in the final part of the book.

2

India's Purse Strings: Union vs States

Origins of India's Fiscal Structure

The Charter Act of 1833 is generally considered the origin of the Indian Union in its current political form. The British Parliament, while extending the Royal Charter to the East India Company through this Act, made the Governor of Bengal the Governor General of India. It took away the powers of legislation and fiscal authority vested with the Governors of Bombay and Madras and subsumed them under the newly created Governor General's office. In effect, the modern Indian Union, including the fiscal union, was created for the convenience and efficiency of the British colonial administration. This Union was further solidified when the British Crown took direct control of India in 1858 after the Revolt of 1857.

In 1860–61, the first budget under the new system was presented for all of India. The budget warranted a clearer delineation of powers between the central and provincial authorities, including the powers of taxation and spending. The Governor General's office took over the powers of taxation for the most part, marking the creation of India's fiscal structure with a prominent skew towards the Centre, which continues to this day. The evolution of this system over the last 160 years has been complicated, but it has also been one of consistent consolidation of the powers of the Centre over its constituent parts.

But even before the first budget was presented, the unfairness and arbitrariness of the system became a point of serious debate – another feature of the system that continues to the present day. Sir Charles Trevelyan, then Governor of the Madras Presidency, raised serious objections to the proposals on taxation. He feared centralization would not be in the interest of the Madras Presidency; large sections of local business and trade interests that opposed the centralized taxation of the professional and service classes frequently met with Governor Trevelyan in 1860, pressing their case. Some sections of the British government even suspected the locals were being instigated by the Governor.

One of the main reasons for the colonial administration to propose new taxes in 1860 was to pay for the war effort during the Revolt of 1857. Sir Trevelyan argued that the Madras Presidency saw little to no disturbance during that war and therefore shouldn't be made to pay for it. He aired his disagreements in public and was arguing for the principle of representation in taxation. It came so uncomfortably close to questioning the rationale of British rule that the colonial government had no option but to recall him. Ironically, though, Sir Trevelyan returned a couple of years later as India's finance minister and implemented some of the taxes he'd opposed as a Governor.

Charles Trevelyan is remembered today largely for his role in worsening the Irish famine that killed a million people. It's a reputation that's well earned in some ways: he wrote a letter at the height of the famine arguing that the famine was a good way to deal with the excess population.

However, his most serious contribution to government may well have been made when he was Governor of Madras Presidency and raised questions about the centralized Indian Union – or any large federal structure – to which there haven't been satisfactory answers still. He favoured decentralization, arguing that it was both democratically just and administratively more robust. He wanted Indians to have a voice and a seat at the table. It may have come from a colonial administrator with a questionable reputation, but Sir Trevelyan had a point in that overt centralization for the purpose of convenience to a colonial administration was no reason to act. That holds true even when the administration is not colonial, as is now the case.

Evolution of the Fiscal Union

The evolution of the fiscal system in India since 1860 has run through multiple commissions and expert committees. The last significant recommendation on the subject prior to Independence was the Cabinet Mission Plan, which recommended that the states/provinces of British India have near complete fiscal sovereignty in their respective provinces, with a severely restricted Union. It's an idea Governor Trevelyan would have approved of.

It was also an idea that was acceptable to Muhammad Ali Jinnah, who saw it as a step short of Partition. Alas, as we now know, that idea did not come to pass, for complicated political reasons. Jawaharlal Nehru argued for a stronger Union to help his agenda of fighting poverty with industrialization, while B.R. Ambedkar wanted a stronger Union to fight the threat of capture of local and provincial governments by the elite.

Apart from its monopoly on violence, the power of the purse is, after all, the most significant power that a modern government has. The government is a government because it gets to raise taxes and spend that money; this is the primary incentive structure by which we've organized society. And between the local, state and Union governments, the degree of taxation by each layer of government generally determines how much influence that layer of government has in our lives.

One approach is to render the local and state governments entirely dependent on the central or Union government for revenue. This is an approach that works in many smaller and homogeneous countries, but fails with scale and diversity. Another extreme is to offer complete state sovereignty, which may end up making the Union government weak.

The latter is what the Cabinet Mission Plan of 1946 recommended. It's also closer to what most large federal structures in democratic set-ups adopt. The United States and Germany have some version of this, though neither is a perfect example. In India, the founders and the Constituent Assembly explicitly tilted the balance in favour of the Union despite the country being large and diverse. The residual powers of what are not explicitly called state subjects rest with the Union in India. That has meant that with time, the Union has amassed even more powers than originally intended. This was only to be expected, as power is a necessary condition for gaining more power.

Today, the Indian Union owns the buoyant sources of taxation, has the ability to interfere in any subject or policy area, regardless of that being suboptimal, and crowds out the fiscal space of state governments. More crucially, the Union controls the classification of revenues, the methods of classification and the bureaucracy. This power of classification becomes everything when it can decide what kind of revenue is to be shared between the Union and the states and what needn't.

Even in the case of those revenues that need to be shared, the Union gets to set the rules of how that revenue gets shared among the states. As a result, the Union not only has the balance tipped in its favour but also gets to arbitrarily change the rules and shift goalposts.

Vertical Imbalance

The Union government currently receives roughly two-thirds of all the tax revenue raised, while being responsible for just over a third of all expenses. Even those expenditures, for the most part, are in areas that are either explicitly state subjects, or areas the Union usurped from states. The Union spends a rather small ratio of its overall expenditure on the core functions of the Union government, such as defence and foreign affairs.

The states, meanwhile, are responsible for close to two-thirds of all expenses while they receive only a third of the revenue directly. That is, the revenue capacity and fiscal responsibility aren't evenly matched between the layers of government. This basic skew, called vertical imbalance, is by design in a federal structure. The theory is that the Union owns the mobile sources of revenue – such as corporate and personal income taxes, for example – so that states do not get into unhealthy competition amongst themselves. And, typically, these mobile sources of revenue are also the most buoyant, making the Union accrue most of the revenue in the country.

But the state and local governments, by virtue of owning the last-mile government services, are responsible for much of the actual governance. To resolve this imbalance, some mechanism for transfer of revenues from the Union to the states exists in most federal structures. Striking a balance between the extent of the original imbalance and the degree of fiscal transfer required to solve it often determines how effective that federal structure is. It's easy to overdo the skew towards the Centre such that local governance suffers.

A rule of thumb that economists use for achieving this balance is to make the vertical transfer such that the richest state is able to bridge the gap between all its expenses and its own tax revenues with the help of transfers from the Union. The logic is that it limits the overall scale of vertical transfer to an effective minimum on the transfer side while restricting the Union government's revenue generation on the collection side by making the liability finite.

It also ensures that states depend on the Union for as little as possible in the process of discharging their duties. There may be poorer states that need greater assistance, but that is an entirely different problem – called horizontal imbalance – and is equalized differently. For the purpose of determining the degree of advantage the Union should have over the states, this rule of thumb for correcting vertical imbalance works reasonably well.

In India, transfer of revenues from the Union to the states happens for the most part under three major buckets: through Finance Commission transfers, through discretionary grants, and through centrally sponsored schemes. The Finance Commission sets the ratio of taxes to be shared with states periodically, every five years. That is, it determines the extent of devolution to the states from the Union to address the vertical imbalance.

The Fourteenth Finance Commission, whose

recommendations were implemented from 2015 through 2020, increased the share of states in the divisible pool of taxes – as part of correcting the vertical imbalance – from 32 per cent to 42 per cent. That is, the Union was supposed to share an additional 10 percentage points of all the taxes it raised with the states, from the previous five-year period.

Finance Commissions, over the years, have been recommending an increased ratio of vertical transfer. They have also sought a higher quantum of the overall transfer through formulaic methods routed through state budgets, as opposed to handing them out as discretionary grants. In the years after Independence, the majority of the grants were routed through the Planning Commission for specific projects. That meant these grants had no common rationale and often went to the politically important states.

To move away from such arbitrary grants on political considerations is partly why the Finance Commissions have sought to increase vertical devolution. Another reason, of course, is that the Finance Commissions have realized that these untied transfers actually make the state governments more effective and efficient. Funds that are tied to a specific project have constraints as to how that money gets spent; these constraints are often set in Delhi and end up adding layers of red tape without necessarily caring much for end delivery.

Despite the increased devolution ratios in the recent Finance Commission recommendations, the overall transfers from the Union to the states did not register a commensurate increase. In 2010–11, at the beginning of the Thirteenth Finance Commission period, the Union transfers were 62 per cent of gross tax revenues. In the ten-year period that followed, every year had a lower ratio of Union transfer of gross tax revenues compared to that starting point. This despite the fact that from 2015, there was supposed to have been a quantum jump owing to a higher mandated vertical transfer. In 2020-21, that ratio was 60 per cent (see Table 1).

Table 1: Union Transfers as % of Gross Tax Revenue

Financial Year	Union Transfers as % of Gross Tax Revenue
2010–11	62.1
2011–12	60.6
2012–13	55.1
2013–14	53.7
2014–15	53.6
2015–16	56.1
2016–17	56.1
2017–18	58.3
2018–19	58.3
2019–20	57.6
2020–21	59.7

Note: Revised Estimates (RE) 2019–20 and Budget Estimates (BE) 2020–21
Source: Fifteenth Finance Commission of India

That is, a higher ratio of the Union's overall taxes somehow managed to yield lower actual transfers! And this has been the tragedy of India's lagging vertical devolution, which shows up as poor last-mile governance.

The data shows that as the Finance Commission mandated a higher transfer the Union drastically slashed other transfers, such as discretionary grants to states (see Table 2). This helped keep the overall ratio of transfers from the Union at a rough constant, defeating the purpose of the Finance Commission's increased vertical devolution.

Table 2: FC vs Non-FC Transfers as % of Union Transfers

Financial year	Total FC Transfers (%)	Non FC Transfers (%)
2010–11	51	49
2011–12	56	45
2012–13	59	41
2013–14	61	39
2014–15	60	40
2015–16	72	28
2016–17	73	27
2017–18	68	32
2018–19	71	30
2019–20	63	38
2020–21	65	35

Note: Revised Estimates (RE) 2019–20 and Budget Estimates (BE) 2020–21
Source: Fifteenth Finance Commission of India

India's Purse Strings: Union vs States

Towards the later years of the Fourteenth Finance Commission period, the Union even managed to bring down the ratio of overall transfers through clever accounting, over and above tinkering with discretionary grants. In 2011–12, the share of the divisible pool – taxes collected in the bucket that the Union has to share with states as recommended by the Finance Commission – was close to 90 per cent of the gross tax revenue. In 2019–20, it was about 70 per cent. That is, the share of taxes the Union is mandated to give the states shrank by about 20 percentage points in the decade when the ratio of taxes to be shared was increased by 10 percentage points!

It's no wonder, therefore, that despite the mandate for higher devolution, the actual quantum of transfers did not change much in the past decade. As the Finance Commission increased the numerator of the devolution ratio, the Union decreased the denominator! It is somewhat comical that the Union is allowed to move tax collections around under different buckets to negate any recommendations it doesn't like. But that is the sad reality.

One simple way for the Union to decrease the share of the divisible pool in gross tax collections is to increase the ratio of cesses and surcharges collected. Cesses and surcharges are, after all, taxes by another name. But the collections under these heads do not go into the divisible pool and the Union doesn't have to share them with the states.

Table 3: Cess and Surcharge as % of Gross Tax Revenue of Union Budget

Year	Cess and Surcharge as % of Gross Tax Revenue
2012	10.4
2013	11.7
2014	12.4
2015	13.5
2016	12.2
2017	13.5
2018	13.9
2019	19.9
2020	20.2
2021	19.9

Note: Financial year 2011–12 is represented as 2012. 2019–20 data is Revised Estimate; 2020–21 data is Budget Estimate.
Source: Fifteenth Finance Commission of India

In 2011–12, the share of cesses and surcharges was 10.4 per cent of gross tax revenues; in 2019–20, it was 20.2 per cent (see Table 3). That is, the increase in the share of cesses and surcharges was equal to the quantum of increase in the share of taxes that the Union had to share with states, at 10 percentage points. In other words, the Government of India renamed taxes as cesses to circumvent the Finance Commission mandate, thus robbing states of their rightful revenue.

A classic example of calling a regular tax a cess is the Agriculture and Infrastructure Development Cess (AIDC) that was introduced in the Union budget of 2021–22. The Union government, in the name of rationalization, converted much of the excise duties into AIDC, which had the direct effect of moving much of the taxes on commodities like petroleum products into a cess, which state governments did not get a share of. This, in some cases, forced states to increase state-level taxes on those very products to meet their revenue shortfall. The end consumer ended up paying twice over as a result of these accounting tricks. It has also meant a political war over inflation between the states and the Union. All of this has happened while the Union kept these collections in the name of cess for itself.

The Union's perennial excuse in seeking higher revenue for itself and lower devolution to the states is that it has responsibilities in the areas of defence, internal security and interest payments for its existing borrowings. Some version of this has been cited by every Union government to almost all Finance Commissions.

But a simple look at how and where the Union spends its revenue punctures this argument. The Union spends about 5 per cent of GDP on defence, security and interest payments combined (see Table 4). It spends more than twice this amount, approximately 12 per cent of GDP, on revenue expenditure, which often encroaches on state subjects and states' rights.

Table 4: Union Government Expenditure of GDP

Year	Revenue Expenditure (%)	Interest Payments (%)	Pay (%)	Pension (%)	Defence (%)	Subsidies (%)	Capital Expenditure (%)	Total (%)
2011–12	13.1	3.1	1.1	0.7	2.0	2.5	1.8	14.9
2012–13	12.5	3.1	1.1	0.7	1.8	2.6	1.7	14.2
2013–14	12.2	3.3	1.0	0.7	1.8	2.3	1.7	13.9
2014–15	11.8	3.2	1.1	0.8	1.8	2.1	1.6	13.3
2015–16	11.2	3.2	1.0	0.7	1.6	1.9	1.8	13.0
2016–17	11.0	3.1	1.2	0.9	1.6	1.5	1.8	12.8
2017–18	11.0	3.1	1.1	0.9	1.6	1.3	1.5	12.5
2018–19	10.6	3.1	1.1	0.8	1.5	1.2	1.6	12.2
2019–20	11.5	3.1	1.2	0.9	1.5	1.3	1.7	13.2
2020–21	11.7	3.1	1.1	0.9	1.4	1.2	1.8	13.5

Source: Fifteenth Finance Commission of India

The Union's budget estimate for 2021–22 for all the centrally sponsored schemes was about Rs 3.81 lakh crore (1 lakh crore = 1 trillion). In contrast, the total Finance Commission transfers, including grants, amounted to only Rs 2.2 lakh-crore. That is, the Union today spends 173 per cent more on centrally sponsored schemes than on the transfers to states mandated by the Finance Commission. Many of these centrally sponsored schemes, though, happen to be programmes focused on what are explicitly state subjects, or those on the Concurrent List. In most instances, there is no good reason for the Union to spend that directly; these programmes – most of them in the areas of health, education, agriculture and social welfare – are better designed and administered by state governments.

After all, the problems in each of these areas are so vastly different across the various states. To have one centrally sponsored scheme with a centrally defined criterion for success and failure is suboptimal, as seen in the previous sections. Yet that's what the Union spends a significant part of its revenue on, rather than sharing it with the states and letting democratically elected state governments decide their priorities for themselves.

Union and State Finances

The Union government thus receives most of the tax revenue and spends it unwisely by itself instead of sharing it with the states as it is supposed to. The argument Union governments over the years have consistently used to defend their actions is that state governments are fiscally profligate and populist. The populism argument is so pervasive that it was even part of the terms of reference of the Fifteenth Finance Commission.

The Union is the implicit guarantor of all debt that's taken on by state and local governments. After all, the market does assume that the Government of India will bail out any state should it default on its loans. But that has become ingrained in the way Union governments think.

The Finance Commission actually cited the argument that Union governments seek to restrict the populism of state governments and improve state-level budget management and that these are factors to consider when deciding on the allocation ratios for states! The idea of the Union getting to tell states they are being profligate with what's rightfully their money, and in the process seeking to keep those monies for itself, is tragi-comic.

If the Union's accusation were true, we would see clear revenue deficits showing up in state budgets. However, a simple look at the historical trends in the combined state-level revenue deficits and the Union's own revenue deficit points to the Union as being far more fiscally profligate than the states (see Table 5).

This has been particularly the case in the first decade and a half of the twenty-first century, when states had entirely eliminated their revenue deficits by 2016. In the years since 2016, with the passing of the GST Bill and the subsequent

Table 5: Revenue Deficit of Centre and States

Year	Revenue Deficit of Union (% of GDP)	Revenue Deficit of States (% of GDP)
1981	1.4	−1.0
1982	0.2	−0.8
1983	0.7	−0.5
1984	1.1	−0.1
1985	1.6	0.4
1986	2.0	−0.2
1987	2.4	−0.1
1988	2.5	0.3
1989	2.4	0.4
1990	2.4	0.7
1991	3.2	0.9
1992	2.4	0.8
1993	2.4	0.7
1994	3.7	0.4
1995	3.0	0.6
1996	2.4	0.7
1997	2.3	1.2
1998	3.0	1.1
1999	3.7	2.5
2000	3.3	2.7
2001	3.9	2.5
2002	4.3	2.6
2003	4.3	2.3
2004	3.5	2.2
2005	2.4	1.2
2006	2.5	0.2
2007	1.9	−0.6
2008	1.1	−0.9
2009	4.5	−0.2
2010	5.2	0.5

Year	Revenue Deficit of Union (% of GDP)	Revenue Deficit of States (% of GDP)
2011	3.2	0.0
2012	4.5	−0.3
2013	3.7	−0.2
2014	3.2	0.1
2015	2.9	0.4
2016	2.5	0.0

Source: Data circulated by the annual publications titled 'Handbook of Statistics on Indian States' by the Reserve Bank of India

pandemic, the finances of both the Union and states have been severely impacted and are in a state of flux, and state deficits are rising again.

The Fiscal Responsibility and Budget Management (FRBM) Act sets a limit of 3 per cent of GDP on the central fiscal deficit. However, the Union has overshot this limit threefold. The fiscal deficit for 2020–21 was 9.5 per cent of GDP. At the same time, the Act has laid down stringent conditions for states to be able to borrow. And in the same budget, the Union government sought to relax the deficit limits for itself citing the pandemic, while extending no such favours to states.

The general yardstick for profligacy that both the Union government and the Finance Commission like to tout is capital expenditure as a ratio of GDP or GSDP. Even by that standard, states do a better job – a consistently and significantly better job, at that (see Table 6).

Table 6: Capital Expenditure of States vs Union

Year	Aggregate Capital Expenditure of States (% of GDP)	Capital Capital Expenditure of Union (% of GDP)
2011–12	2.4	1.8
2012–13	2.2	1.7
2013–14	2.2	1.7
2014–15	2.4	1.6
2015–16	3.1	1.8
2016–17	3.3	1.8
2017–18	2.5	1.5
2018–19	2.5	1.6
2019–20	2.7	1.7

Source: Fifteenth Finance Commission of India

States have also managed better tax buoyancy – that is, they earned more revenue for a commensurate increase in the rate of taxation – than the Union. This has happened despite the Union cornering the mobile and buoyant sources of tax revenue for itself.

Accounting, the basic truth that financial disputes are argued upon, has been another victim of the Union's monopoly on taxes. It has never been transparent as to how net proceeds – that is, gross tax revenue minus the cost of collecting taxes – have been calculated.

The Comptroller and Auditor General of India (CAG) mentioned this in its 2016 report as well. More specifically, this lack of transparency means states do not know how the revenue accrued in the divisible pool is calculated. In 2016, the CAG found an aggregate shortfall of over Rs 81,000 crore in the divisible pool for the previous fifteen years. That a modern republic allows such a lapse in basic accounting is shocking.

In effect, the vertical imbalance in India's fiscal structure, which was skewed in favour of the Union to begin with, has exponentially worsened in the time since Independence. And the trend has only worsened in the past decade. The Union sets the rules of the game in which it is a player itself; it gets to arbitrarily reclassify taxes as 'cess' and not share that revenue with states; it gets to set limits on the fiscal deficits in state budgets while not adhering to those limits in its own budget; it gets to do worse on most measures of fiscal prudence while lecturing states on fiscal profligacy; and, above all, it gets to set policy and programmes that states must spend their budgetary resources on despite not having designed those policies or programmes themselves.

Horizontal Imbalance

The funds the Union shares with states – the vertical transfers mandated by the Finance Commission – are shared with each state based on the Finance Commission's allocation for each. The Finance Commission's biggest lever of power, apart from deciding the ratio of vertical devolution, is its ability to decide how much each state gets within that vertical devolution. States, through transfers mandated by the Finance Commission, get untied budgetary transfers from the divisible pool and specific grants for specific sectors and projects (see Table 7). That allocation ratio amongst states is used to address the horizontal imbalance between them.

Table 7: Total Transfers Recommended by the Fifteenth Finance Commission

State	Share in Central Taxes and Duties (Values in Crore)	Total Grants in Aid (Values in Crore)
Andhra Pradesh	1,70,976	63,037
Assam	1,32,152	37,611
Bihar	4,24,926	53,825
Chhattisgarh	1,43,938	17,231
Gujarat	1,46,938	37,216
Haryana	46,177	16,921
Himachal Pradesh	35,064	46,913
Jharkhand	1,39,712	19,919
Karnataka	1,54,077	38,437
Kerala	81,326	55,618
Madhya Pradesh	3,31,642	50,368
Maharashtra	2,66,877	70,375
Odisha	1,91,297	31,262
Punjab	76,343	43,996
Rajasthan	2,54,583	59,374
Tamil Nadu	1,72,329	40,351
Telangana	88,806	20,980
Uttar Pradesh	7,57,879	97,121
West Bengal	3,17,828	86,481

Source: Fifteenth Finance Commission of India

The rationale for this horizontal devolution is to provide a levelling effect. For instance, the mountainous states of

India's northeast aren't densely populated and won't have a sufficient population base to raise their own revenue, as other states do. The share of taxes collected by the Union from states with a lower base will also likely be low. Thus, a direct application of the vertical devolution ratio on taxes collected in regions that do not have a sufficient tax base may not be appropriate. The Finance Commission, the constitutionally mandated equalizer of sorts, recommends allocations, ratios and grants for each state to fix that imbalance (see Table 8).

Table 8: Inter se Shares of States (Allocation Ratio for Horizontal Devolution Recommended by the Fifteenth Finance Commission)

State	Inter se Shares (%)
Andhra Pradesh	4.05
Assam	3.13
Bihar	10.06
Chhattisgarh	3.41
Gujarat	3.48
Haryana	1.09
Himachal Pradesh	0.83
Jharkhand	3.31
Karnataka	3.65
Kerala	1.93
Madhya Pradesh	7.85
Maharashtra	6.32
Odisha	4.53
Punjab	1.81
Rajasthan	6.03
Tamil Nadu	4.08
Telangana	2.10

State	Inter se Shares (%)
Uttar Pradesh	17.94
West Bengal	7.52

Source: Fifteenth Finance Commission of India

The Fifteenth Finance Commission's allocation ratios and the actual recommended fund transfers to address horizontal imbalance – particularly the processes by which the ratios were arrived at – marked a distinct turn in the way in which Finance Commissions perceived, and more importantly were asked to look at, resource allocation problems in India. Finance Commissions are typically given 'terms of reference' (TOR) by the Union government. These TORs serve as the basic framework through which Finance Commissions look at the resource allocation problems they aim to solve.

The Fifteenth Finance Commission was the first to be asked to consider population data from the 2011 census entirely. The previous Finance Commissions took the 1971 census, the last census before population planning became a national policy, as their primary reference. As seen in the previous chapters, this shift to using population data from 2011 to allocate resources punishes states that did well in population control and incentivizes those that did not.

Further, the TOR reads like a laundry list of the Union government's policy preferences. For example, the TOR asks the Finance Commission to consider states' adoption of direct benefit transfer, their implementation of GST and their implementation of centrally sponsored schemes. It also asks it to consider limiting states' 'populist' expenditure.

None of these need to be the priorities of a state government. That the Union government gets to impose these criteria on states towards determining how much revenue they get back from the Union is how the original skew towards the Union has grown to absurd proportions. The tax money, after all, belongs to the states as much as it belongs to the Union.

Consider the TOR's intent to penalize state governments for 'populism'. There was no explicit definition of what constituted populism. If it's ballooning revenue deficits or a low capital expenditure ratio, it is the state governments that need to rein in the Union, if anything, and not vice versa. If it is programmes and policies that do not have proper evaluation methods, it is the centrally sponsored schemes, which are impossible to monitor, that need to be stopped. But somehow, the Union gets to set the terms for sharing resources with the states against the very parameters that it has done poorly on. Unfortunately, vertical devolution and horizontal devolution of tax revenues have become instruments of political power in the hands of the Union. The government with greater resources and a greater control of those larger resources is after all the more powerful government! And the politicians who control that layer of government end up being the more powerful politicians. The Union thus uses the levers under its control to maximize the revenue at its disposal and minimize the flow of untied fund transfers to states. The idea of a Union government telling an elected state government what is good and what is populist defeats the purpose of having duly elected state governments. But that's where we are.

Predictably, the TOR for the Fifteenth Finance Commission, when it was first published, resulted in a political backlash. The mandated use of 2011 census data was the biggest point of contention. The finance ministers of several states got together and objected to that and to some other terms that the Finance Commission was asked to consider for horizontal devolution. This was also repeatedly reinforced in the representations to the Finance Commission made by state after state when the Commission met with the state-level political leadership in their consultations. In response, the chairman of the Fifteenth Finance Commission repeatedly assured states and concerned citizens that there'd be a balancing act. He promised the introduction of demographic performance as a factor that would neutralize the effect of considering the census 2011 data.

When the final report of the Fifteenth Finance Commission with its allocation ratios for each state and the methodology used were released, it was worse than what the TOR had threatened for states in southern India. Demographic performance as a factor to be considered, promised as a compensation for considering the 2011 population data instead of the 1971 data – had little to no effect on the report. The Finance Commission, bizarrely, scaled the very factor that was supposed to counteract the 2011 population data using 2011 population data. This made state demographic performance as a factor pale in relevance. Not just that, every other factor that went into deciding the allocation ratio was also scaled using 2011 population data!

Table 9: Weights Assigned to Different Criteria under Horizontal Devolution for the the Fifteenth Finance Commission

Criteria	Weight (%)
Population	15.0
Area	15.0
Forest and Ecology	10.0
Income Distance	45.0
Tax and Fiscal Efforts	2.5
Demographic Performance	12.5

Source: Fifteenth Finance Commission

The weightage the Finance Commission assigned for population and demographic performance, when one reads the main report, looks like a reasonable compromise. Assigning 15 per cent weightage to 2011 population data but assigning 12.5 per cent weightage to demographic performance sounds like a good way to counteract the demographic divergence of the last half century among states, for example (see Table 9).

The annexures reveal why this isn't much of a balancing act at all. The twist lies in what the Finance Commission has used for calculating demographic performance. It has taken the inverse of TFR in 2011 and multiplied that with the population figures for 1971. In other words, the parameter that was explicitly supposed to be about population control has been scaled against absolute population figures!

The result is that the very criterion supposed to reward demographic performance and punish lack of population control measures gives states with the highest populations in 2011 the maximum scores, based on those very factors. Uttar Pradesh – the state with the largest population and with above-replacement TFR still – scored the highest for demographic performance! This defeated the very purpose of introducing that metric (see Table 10).

Table 10: Inter se Shares for Demographic Performance, Fifteenth Finance Commission

Demographic performance: factor for rewarding states with low TFR in the horizontal devolution allocation criteria of the 15th FC

State	*Inter se Shares for Demographic Performance (%)*
Andhra Pradesh	6.64
Assam	2.60
Bihar	5.51
Chhattisgarh	1.84
Gujarat	5.04
Haryana	1.66
Himachal Pradesh	0.76
Jharkhand	2.09
Karnataka	6.21
Kerala	4.57
Madhya Pradesh	4.38
Maharashtra	10.12
Odisha	4.25
Punjab	2.79
Rajasthan	3.53
Tamil Nadu	10.00
Telangana	3.63
Uttar Pradesh	12.32
West Bengal	10.11

Source: Finance Commission of India

The biggest criterion for deciding the overall allocation ratio in the Fifteenth Finance Commission's report is income distance. One may agree or disagree on the merits of having 45 per cent of the total weightage assigned to income distance. But income distance in the way it's calculated is again basically a proxy for population.

Income distance has been calculated as the distance of a given state's per capita GSDP, taken over a three-year period, from that of Haryana (India's third-wealthiest state). So far it seems reasonable. Except that this distance is then scaled using the 2011 population of each state! The end result, much like that of demographic performance, renders income distance another proxy for the population figures of 2011 (see Table 11).

Table 11: Income Distance – Inter se Share

State	Income Distance
Andhra Pradesh	3
Assam	4
Bihar	16
Chhattisgarh	3
Gujarat	2
Haryana	0
Himachal Pradesh	0
Jharkhand	4
Karnataka	1
Kerala	1
Madhya Pradesh	9
Maharashtra	3
Odisha	5

State	Income Distance
Punjab	2
Rajasthan	7
Tamil Nadu	2
Telangana	1
Uttar Pradesh	27
West Bengal	10

Source: Fifteenth Finance Commission of India

Unsurprisingly, both demographic performance and income distance, amounting to a combined weightage of 57.5 per cent, are correlated more to population than to their respective criterion definitions. Their correlation with population is very high, simply because the scaling factor dominates that calculation by virtue of being a much larger number than the actual factor they are a scale for! This is in addition to another existing factor for population, which accounts for 15 per cent weightage. Thus, about 72.5 per cent of the overall weightage in the horizontal devolution criteria either explicitly favours the high-population states or is a proxy favouring high-population states. Worse, all of it is based on the 2011 population data.

Finance Commissions over the years have dealt a blow to the southern states in particular when it comes to horizontal devolution. The five southern states, by virtue of their low population growth rates and higher levels of urbanization, have lost out the most, given the set of criteria chosen by each of the Finance Commissions in the twenty-first century thus far.

Kerala's allocation ratio, for instance, has dropped the most between the Twelfth and Fifteenth Finance Commissions' recommendations – from 2.67 per cent to 1.93 per cent (see Table 12). That's a drop of 27.7 per cent in two decades for the state. Tamil Nadu follows next, with a loss of 23.1 per cent in its share over the same period. Karnataka and the erstwhile unified Andhra Pradesh follow at third and fourth positions. This is how India punishes states that achieve low TFR and relative prosperity – by massively cutting their financial resources.

Table 12: Change in Allocation Ratio of Horizontal Devolution between Twelfth and Fifteenth Finance Commissions

State	Change from Twelfth to Fifteenth Finance Commission (%)
Andhra Pradesh (unified, including Telangana)	−16.4
Assam	−3.3
Bihar	−8.8
Chhattisgarh	28.4
Gujarat	−2.6
Haryana	1.7
Himachal Pradesh	59.0
Jharkhand	−1.6
Karnataka	−18.2
Kerala	−27.8
Madhya Pradesh	17.0
Maharashtra	26.4
Odisha	−12.3

India's Purse Strings: Union vs States

State	Change from Twelfth to Fifteenth Finance Commission (%)
Punjab	39.1
Rajasthan	7.4
Tamil Nadu	−23.1
Uttar Pradesh	−6.9
West Bengal	6.6

Source: Twelfth and Fifteenth Finance Commissions of India

Another way to understand India's fiscal structure is to look at how much the states are spending in their annual budgets relative to their respective GSDPs (see Chart 1). All central transfers that are routed through state budgets show up on their budgets by definition, after all.

Chart 1: GSDP vs Budget Expenditure, 2018–19

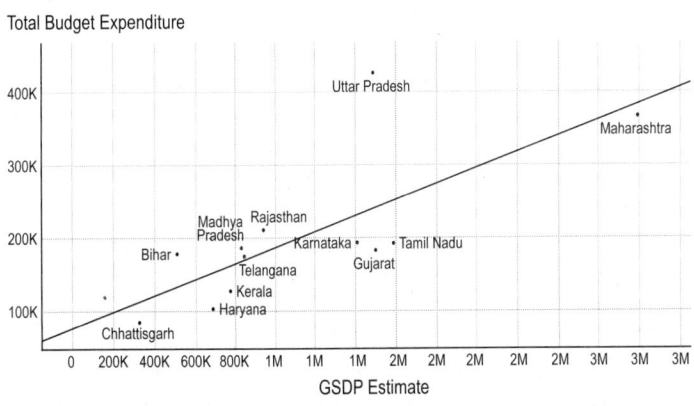

Sources: Various state governments

A simple regression plot of GSDP vs budget shows up the imbalance quite obviously: Uttar Pradesh is an extreme outlier, in the sense that it consumes financial resources that are way more than what its GSDP entails. The state has a positive residual that's an order of magnitude bigger than those of other states. That is, what most of the richer states pay into the federal system goes to Uttar Pradesh. States like Tamil Nadu, Gujarat, Karnataka and Kerala have state budgets that are much smaller than what their GSDPs would warrant, as the plot reveals.

Uttar Pradesh is in the opposite situation: that is, its state budget is much, much larger than its GSDP warrants. This is not so much a problem for Uttar Pradesh as for the other states, which pay in. It's perfectly reasonable for people in other states to wonder why their tax money has to fund the budget of Uttar Pradesh while their own state hasn't funded its basic government services fully.

One of the effects of this skewed horizontal devolution is that it ends up placing twice the burden of resources on citizens from some states (see Table 13).

Consider Telangana: the state's own tax revenue was 7.7 per cent of its GSDP for 2020–21, while central transfers accounted for only 2.5 per cent of GSDP. That is, the state received so little from the Union that it was forced to tax its citizens at the state level.

In contrast, Bihar got 31 per cent of its GSDP as central transfers for the same period. This partly reveals the tragedy of Bihar; the state's economy is so lopsided and its GSDP

Table 13: States' Own Taxes and Transfers from Union, 2020–21 BE

State	On Tax Revenue (% of GSDP)	Total Transfers from Union (% of GSDP)	Total Transfers from Union – Own Tax Revenue (% of GSDP)
Andhra Pradesh	7.0	8.5	1.5
Assam	5.7	15.0	9.3
Bihar	5.1	31.0	25.9
Chhattisgarh	7.2	13.4	6.2
Gujarat	5.8	2.0	−3.8
Haryana	5.5	2.4	−3.1
Himachal Pradesh	6.0	14.0	8.0
Jharkhand	5.7	10.9	5.2
Karnataka	6.2	3.3	−2.9
Kerala	6.9	3.3	−3.6
Madhya Pradesh	5.1	8.3	3.2
Maharashtra	7.0	3.2	−3.8
Odisha	5.9	10.5	4.6
Punjab	5.6	6.8	1.2
Rajasthan	6.8	6.8	0.0
Tamil Nadu	6.4	3.3	−3.1
Telangana	7.7	2.5	−5.2
Uttar Pradesh	9.3	12.6	3.3
Uttarakhand	4.7	8.6	3.9
West Bengal	4.9	7.2	2.3

Source: Fifteenth Finance Commission of India

so low that the central transfers amount to such a large ratio of it. But it also points to how the burden of taxation across states is uneven in the extreme.

The states' own revenues as a per cent of GSDP are consistently high for all the peninsular states since they have relatively lower rates of population growth and lower rates of poverty. That is, people in these states are taxed more heavily than others – first in the form of Union taxes, simply because those taxes target them better; and second, by the states in which they live, which tax them more as the Union taxes are mostly sent elsewhere. This is on top of the Union masking some taxes as cesses, which only worsens the tax burden for people in these states.

Union transfers to states are not just through state budgets, though. The Union government runs its own welfare programmes, subsidy programmes, et al., bypassing state governments. These are often bigger than state programmes, and this spending too is skewed in favour of the more populated and more rural states in central and northern India, making the existing imbalances worse.

India's Unique Pickle

Fiscal imbalance between different regions of a country is a common enough phenomenon worldwide. Most large federal structures have some version of it, which is corrected through tax policy. In the United States, for example, the southern part of the country has been poorer than the industrial north for a very long time. Consequently, the federal government equalizes the situation among regions by sending more federal dollars to the south. In Germany, the western part of the country is still significantly wealthier than the erstwhile communist east. The federal structure in Germany again balances financial resources somewhat between the regions.

This dynamic is true for countries as vastly diverse as Spain, China and the United Kingdom, and many others. But two important differences exist between those countries and India. The first is that the contrast between the regions in those countries isn't as wide as it is in India. The second and more important difference is: in those countries, the more prosperous regions are also the more populous regions that happen to be more urbanized and have a higher population growth than the poorer regions owing to greater inflows from migration. Whereas in India, it's the poorer regions that are more populous and have high population growth because of their higher TFRs. Unlike in those countries, in India it is TFR that drives population growth and not migration.

Consider the states of New York or California in the United States. They are relatively large, prosperous and historically attractive places for people from the rural parts of the American south or Midwest to migrate to. The prosperous coastal states of that country have a population growth that far exceeds that of the poorer states in Appalachia, for example; in fact, many areas in America's rural middle have negative population growth. TFR across all these sets of states is roughly the same, though. The difference in population growth between these states is entirely explained by the migration of people from the poorer regions to the economic centres in search of better opportunities.

This is true even in China, where a one-child policy for over a generation meant there are no differences in TFR among its provinces. In these countries, the more populous regions are giving up some of their wealth to less prosperous and less populated regions that are further depopulating. Hence, this doesn't show up as a significant problem. The rich states can afford it, and it doesn't have a cascading effect.

In India, the problem is, the relatively prosperous states are also the states with a lower population base and happen to have lower population growth rates too. In some cases, they are even set to experience depopulation in the near future. They are funding states with a much higher population base and with a much higher population growth rate too. Telangana trying to equalize Uttar Pradesh is the equivalent of sticking a finger in a dyke, in some senses. This is a strategy that demands too much from those willing to help, and almost goads the people receiving help into performing poorly.

The states in the peninsular south paying for the sparsely populated northeast, for example, is comparable to what happens in other countries. But in India these states are equalizing Uttar Pradesh, a state of over 200 million, and Bihar, a state of over 100 million. These two states together have a population that's much greater than all the southern states combined.

For the southern states to subsidize the much larger states in the northern and central plains of India is an impossible task if their own growth is also a consideration. And we may note that these southern states aren't wealthy by global standards; they are merely better off compared to the rest of India.

The Finance Commission promised to consider demographic performance as a counter for considering population for allocation of resources. Yet, as seen above, roughly three-quarters of all the weightage has been assigned to population. Firstly, that's a betrayal of trust. Secondly, the way in which the calculations were made – particularly the scaling of metrics against the 2011 population numbers – is amateurish for a policy solution to a serious resource allocation issue affecting 20 per cent of the world's population. If the consequences weren't so enormous, this incompetence in methodology would be considered amusing.

Above all, the current allocation is undemocratic. Most citizens in India's southern states would agree to some equalization, as a matter of principle. It's the extreme nature of it that makes it problematic. The parameters are set arbitrarily, as if to punish success. Citizens pay taxes and vote to elect their governments so as to decide how to use that tax money. They seek to influence policies on health, education and local administration so as to improve the way in which their society is run. The taxes that citizens in these southern states pay, though, are subject to a fulcrum that shifts much of them to the northern plains and violates that basic social contract of a liberal democracy.

What the Finance Commission allocations, the centrally sponsored schemes and the fiscal structure of India do is break the virtuous cycle of democratic kinship at the subnational level, especially in southern India. The taxes collected here are moved elsewhere for the most part. Programmes in the areas of health and education are designed at the national level by the Union government and do not serve local populations well. The policy goals also often have no regard for achievements that have already far exceeded those goals.

As the Union usurps the states' functions, it systematically destroys the bond that citizens have with their immediate society. In the Union's defence, it is seeking to create this bond at the national level. But at the level of 1.3 billion people, that is risking what is sacred, and what works, for what's practically global and likely to fail.

3

Can the Indian Union Be Salvaged in Its Current Form?

India's states are disparate and divergent in the extreme, as the data on health, education and economy reveals. In health, the difference between the best and worst states is as wide as that between the OECD countries and sub-Saharan Africa. In education, it's as wide as that between middle-income and low-income countries. In terms of economic prospects, the better-off states are two to three times richer than the poorest. Overall, southern India is a vastly different place from central and northern India.

The degree of divergence of India's states demands policymaking and fiscal sovereignty at the state level for effective governance. After all, it's impossible for one entity to make a single policy decision that can apply equally effectively to both Afghanistan and the United States in health, for example. But India's Union government is increasingly trying to assume such an impossible role.

The solutions to the problems of these various societies and states, as the previous part details, are often ones that are orthogonal to each other, given their developmental trajectories. For example, the southern states need to focus on output metrics in education while the northern states need to get children into school and keep them there. The southern states need to focus on chronic health issues and possibly elder care, given their demographics and current achievements, while the northern states need to focus on pre- and postnatal healthcare delivery. These differences seep into almost all areas of public policy, making any centralized policy unwieldy and impossible to implement.

In this scenario of increasing divergence in development and governance metrics, the additional complicating factor of divergence in population growth makes a difficult problem impossible to solve. The population skew towards the states in the Indo-Gangetic plains, which also happen to be poorer and less developed, has created a problem that's unique to India in some ways. The less developed states have more political power, owing to their larger populations, and they are threatening to accrue even more political power to themselves in the near future, thereby cornering more resources for themselves and starving the states that are doing well.

The southern states are caught in this peculiar bind: they are doing well because they have achieved stable populations through good governance, which is exactly what threatens to rob them of political power and resource allocation. And this threat fructifies precisely at a time their citizens have come to expect relatively better government services from their states and are seeking to customize them even further to their changing needs.

Consider Telangana. Data shows the state has the highest negative differential in its budget between the amount of money it receives from the Union versus the money it raises from its own citizens via state taxes. That is, its citizens pay the most into state taxes because their share of the Union transfers isn't enough to run the state government. This increasing burden of taxation is placed on the citizens of Telangana while, simultaneously, their democratic power to influence that decision-making is under threat of being diluted.

This is a question with no easy answers for the southern states. The status quo condemns them to receiving less in transfers, giving more in taxes and sacrificing political power – all because they have been successful. The southern states also happen to be linguistically and culturally distinct from the north, which adds a whole new dimension of political complexity. The definition of a nation – a linguistically and culturally distinct people living in a geographically contiguous region – applies to these states better than to most European countries.

One simplistic, risky and often unviable option that has been considered in the past in this country and in several other countries too is the politics of explicit secession. That often hardens stances on both sides and descends into violence.

It's a high-risk option that probably isn't a good solution in the first place. Divergence within a large system is a symptom of structural flaws. A simple realignment of the map with the same structure of governance is likely to yield the same problem downstream in two countries instead of in one, even if the secession magically did not descend into violence.

A democratically just way of organizing society into layers that will solve resource allocation issues and sidestep the perverse incentives for population growth is difficult to arrive at. The next part of the book will analyse the existing structure of government and consider the possible ways in which one may arrive at a stable, peaceful and just system that accurately represents the will of the people at all levels.

Part III
A More Perfect Union

Introduction: Imagining a Better Union

The Indian Union, as seen in the previous parts of the book, is too diverse to be governed by the same set of centralized policies if the goal is to have a democratically just order that values each citizen equally. The divergence of India's states across a wide set of indicators makes that glaringly obvious.

The Union, though, is tending towards such a unitary, centralized government, however unstable that option may be. This dangerous path that the Indian Union is traversing may even lead to civil strife and violence; history is replete with those, after all.

To understand why the status quo is tending towards such an unstable and possibly dangerous situation, it's useful to investigate representative democracy as it is practised in India and to explore the incentives of the system, as well as its flaws, and think of possible alternatives.

India was set up as a Union of states for historical reasons. It adopted the Westminster system of democracy as an erstwhile British colony. However, the scale of the country magnifies the flaws of that system, given the size of each constituency and its many states with their widely divergent levels of development.

It should be clear to a reader who has come this far that decentralization would lead to better utilitarian outcomes, in that local governments could better craft policy to suit local needs rather than struggle to accommodate one-size-fits-all policies imposed by a central authority.

How individual representatives are elected, how they come together to form a government and how policy gets made after government formation are all elements of the democratic system. But in the Indian model as it now stands, each of those skews the system away from decentralization and closer to a unitary form of government. These elements also weaken transmission of the will of the people.

This final part looks at the current electoral system and how that leads to poor outcomes in many ways. The unviability of the current parliamentary system is one of the reasons for India's seeming unviability. It is also a cause for much anxiety apropos the delimitation dilemma.

Are there options and alternative forms of democracy that will lead to a more just reflection of the people's will? Can we avoid majoritarian chaos and achieve maximal decentralization?

The hope is to build a less imperfect union that seeks to balance the immediate concerns of the day with the long-term project of building a liberal society that delivers better quality of life to everybody. The goal is to march towards enlightened liberalism, but to do so through conservative means to create a stable, just and responsive system of government.

Imagining a Better Union

One proposed alternative, which we can call 'gamified direct democracy', has been discussed at length in the final chapter. This is a blue-sky thought experiment, and it may be politically unfeasible in that it would require politicians who hold policymaking powers under the current system to actually choose to give up those powers. But the proposed solution, if implemented, could yield a decentralized Union that would sidestep some of India's most difficult problems.

1

What Ails India's Representative Democracy?

Democracy's Problem of Scale

Democracy is hard. There's no good way to elect a government that perfectly reflects the will of the people. Even small countries with homogeneous populations struggle with it. The scale of the problem tests the limits of credulity in a country as large, diverse and populous as India. Post-colonial states have an added problem, since their boundaries are often not natural units.

Democracies typically try to solve the problems of legitimating the consent of the governed and reflecting the will of the people through a representative model that holds periodic elections. It's a solution that ranges from being an acceptable approximation to being antithetical to liberal democratic ideals, depending on the context of its implementation. The complicated political situation in Iraq in the twenty-first century after the American invasion, for example, explains why merely holding elections – even if they are free and fair – does not make for an enlightened and/or stable democracy.

The demographic reality of such post-colonial states with unnatural boundaries and traumatic histories often makes the majority choice indistinguishable from majoritarianism. In the Iraqi experience, we have a Shia majority, an elite Sunni minority and pockets of other oppressed minority groups – each with a complicated history of past independent alignments with powerful geopolitical partners, making them all deeply suspicious of each other. This renders any fully unified authority in the conventional sense unfair, and any election to it ineffective.

India, with a population of 1.3 billion – with its multiple ethnic, religious, linguistic and developmental divides and its history of conflicts amongst stakeholders – has a similarly intractable problem. The size and scope of its cleavages makes it exponentially more difficult, if not as acute and urgent as, the problem in Iraq. The structure of administrative power for such a large and diverse population cannot be unitary; but as a corollary the absence of a unitary structure will raise questions about the country's raison d'être.

The purpose of a government is to be a tool of convenience for the people who elect it and not a thing unto itself. Unitary power structures, especially in large and diverse countries with significant minorities, don't meet this criterion.

The first problem in such a complicated environment relates to the efficiency of the electoral system and how that affects the structure of government. The basic question to answer here is whether the government in such a system reflects the will of the people to make the idea of democracy – that of a self-governing people – work as intended.

Consider the way democracy is implemented in India. In this version of the Westminster system, citizens elect MPs to represent them and their constituency. Elected representatives, based on their party's majority in Parliament, form the government. In a multiparty system, this often means coalition governments amongst parties that don't agree on everything. These parties still come together to form a government to implement what they don't disagree on. There are multiple layers of transmission in this process: people choose their representatives; representatives choose a government in what's often likely to be a coalition of sorts; and finally, the government chooses policy with the consent of Parliament.

Very often, there's a more important but invisible fourth layer: individual MPs band together and choose their respective party positions; or, looked at the other way, parties choose positions which individual MPs must adhere to. There is transmission loss at each of these stages and in the transition from one stage to the next when it comes to reflecting the will of the people.

First Past the Post: Good for Horses, Bad for Democracy

The first layer of democracy in India is the most egregious example of transmission loss. MPs represent constituencies that may have up to a couple of million voters. They are elected using a first-past-the-post (FPTP) system in multi-cornered contests, where winners frequently get less than a third of all votes cast. In a constituency with over a million voters and four major contestants, it is frequently the case that the winner gets less than 3,00,000 votes. This is a bad way to elect our representatives, even if we do assume that electing representatives is a desirable way to transmit the will of the people. Transmission is not likely to be efficient if two-thirds of voters in fact voted against the winning candidate. Since this happens on a nationwide scale across constituencies, it is a particularly poor way to represent the will of the people.

For instance, in 2014, the Bharatiya Janata Party (BJP) got about 31 per cent of the popular vote and won 282 of the 543 parliamentary seats to form the government. That is, it won more than half the seats in Parliament by winning less than a third of the vote. Its main opponent, the Congress Party, won 19 per cent of the popular vote and about 8 per cent of all seats. In other words, FPTP not only picks winners in individual constituencies who weren't the choice of the majority of voters, it also frequently over-represents such winners and under-represents losers in Parliament.

What Ails India's Representative Democracy? 217

The basic flaw of FPTP is that the lack of proportionality between winners and losers is exacerbated in a large and diverse country with a multiparty democracy like India. Until recently, the Congress Party, by virtue of being the largest party, had similarly enjoyed outsized representation in Parliament compared to its actual vote share.

The problems with the FPTP system reveal themselves in different ways in different democratic systems, though. In the United States, for example, in the largely two-party, decentralized election process, it ends up incentivizing partisan gerrymandering. That is, partisans who draw the boundaries of their constituencies draw them such that their party wins the maximum number of seats with the minimum number of votes and the minimum margin in each seat.

The arithmetic reality of the FPTP system is that every additional vote polled after the winning vote adds no value while trying to maximize the number of representatives elected. In a two-party system, for example, winning 70 per cent of the votes in a constituency is no different from winning 50.01 per cent of the votes. From the perspective of the political party, those additional 20 per cent votes in those constituencies are 'wasted' if they could have been used elsewhere to win seats.

Say, for example, a political party wins 100 per cent of the vote in one constituency and loses by narrow margins while taking 49 per cent of the vote in three neighbouring constituencies (all of the same size). It would be better if it could somehow transfer at least 6 per cent of its votes from the winning constituency to win the other three too.

Therefore, political consultants in America who help the two major parties determine where these constituency boundaries should be drawn spend enormous resources in determining the most advantageous method for their respective sides. They try to draw the boundaries in such a way that their own party 'wastes' as little votes as possible while winning as many seats as possible.

This idea of making sure the voters are diffused enough for a party to win many seats and not waste votes by pooling them all in a few constituencies is called 'cracking'. The opposite action of ensuring that votes are sufficiently concentrated to ensure victory in a given constituency is called 'packing'.

No party wants its voters so diffused that it wins the popular vote but loses the majority of seats. Partisan consultants try to find an optimal balance between these two possibilities, cracking and packing to ensure outsized victories for their party in terms of number of seats won. This redistricting process has now been elevated to an art and a science, so much so that opposition parties that win the popular vote often end up in the minority because the incumbents get to redistrict each state after the census data is made available every ten years. In effect, this has meant that representatives choose their voters, and not vice versa!

The shape of constituencies in the United States is often as far removed from a circle – a natural compact unit – as possible, owing to such gerrymandering. To stop this, a metric often suggested is the Polsby–Popper score, which measures the area of a constituency as a ratio of the area of a circle with the same perimeter. This tells us how dissimilar the constituency is from a circle; heavily engineered boundaries will result in a very low score. While this geometric ratio is often not the best measure, it's a useful indicator.

Americans have taken this rather obscure problem to egregious and outlandish limits – such as clustering disparate places that should be in four or five different constituencies into one constituency.

In India, partisans, or political operatives, do not redraw boundaries. The Election Commission does that. Even then, some boundaries can raise eyebrows. The Manamadurai and Sulur Assembly constituencies in Tamil Nadu are good examples. They'd get very poor Polsby–Popper scores. It's not clear how and why the Election Commission draws constituency boundaries the way it does. But, even without gerrymandering, this points to a deeper problem: the FPTP system is a winner-takes-all system that is non-proportional in its representation.

Circumventing FPTP

The FPTP system is neither democratic nor just. It does a poor job of electing representatives and is a poor transmission model even if done well. Let's consider some other approaches.

A widely used solution to guard against flaws of the winner-takes-all system is proportional representation (PR).

Countries as disparate as Sri Lanka, Germany, Denmark, New Zealand and Bolivia use it. The way it is implemented is often varied, and with varying effectiveness.

The basic idea, though, is an attempt to make the seats in Parliament reflective of the overall vote split across parties, which is not the case in the winner-takes-all system. This could be achieved by having each constituency represented by more than one member, by adjusting the overall number of seats to reflect the overall vote split, by adjusting the voting weights of each member corresponding to their vote share, or in many other ways.

A criticism of PR is that MPs' connection with their constituencies is weakened if they don't fully represent their constituency. That's not always true, though. In fact, one could argue that it improves the connection in some scenarios. When an MP from one constituency is forced to engage with another MP from the same constituency in the same Parliament, it could even force deeper deliberation.

Another problem of the FPTP system is that it is mutable in a multi-cornered contest. There is no post in FPTP; the winning threshold isn't fixed and can fall absurdly low if there are many viable candidates in the fray. In the absence of PR, therefore, multi-cornered FPTP elections can become a reflection of a minority's choice rather than the majority's will.

A related but different and even more serious problem with the FPTP system, as implemented in India, is that it shifts the onus of tactical voting on citizens, as opposed to what obtains in an electoral system that is robust enough to sift through voters' choices. This often happens in states with triangular or quadrangular contests – like Uttar Pradesh – where voters have to decide between their most preferred candidate and a less liked but more broadly acceptable candidate who is likely to win against a third or fourth candidate the voters absolutely want to see defeated.

In such a scenario, a candidate who wants to vote for, let's say, the Congress Party in Uttar Pradesh, may often end up voting for the Samajwadi Party or the Bahujan Samaj Party in order to defeat the BJP. Or, we may see some other permutation of the above scenario. This is hopelessly complicated. Instead of voters expressing their personal choice, they are trying to think about how others may vote. Pundits who earn a living by trying to explain how people are going to vote routinely get it wrong. As do opinion polls. So, to expect ordinary voters to be able to predict anything before they vote defeats the basic purpose of holding elections.

One simple way to ease this specific problem would be to offer ranked-choice voting, where voters are allowed to rank the candidates in order of their preference. This ranking by each voter can be of the full list of candidates or of a partial list or of even just one chosen candidate. That is, if ten candidates are contesting, a voter could pick just three of them and rank them as options 1, 2 and 3. Or the voter could pick all ten and rank them in order of preference, or pick just one candidate. Once such a ranked-choice ballot is cast, an iteration of the following algorithm (which is used in several European countries) could be used to count the votes:

1. Count all first-preference votes not yet counted.
2. If some party has over 50 per cent of first-preference votes, HALT (that party wins.)
3. If no party crosses 50 per cent, take the party with the smallest number of first-preference votes. In the ballots where that party is the first preference, remove the first-preference votes for that party. Take the second choices on those ballots and promote those into first-preference votes for the other parties,
4. Remove that party from the list of preferences of all other voters.
5. GO TO 1. Calculate again with the newly promoted second-preference votes.
6. Do as many iterations as required to find a winner.

This method will pick the candidate that most people agree on and least disagree on. It would eliminate the need for voters to mentally simulate the choice of other voters when casting their votes. And if someone has a problem with any or every other candidate, they could just restrict their voting-preference count accordingly.

If voters restrict their choice to just one candidate, the system defaults to being FPTP. This method of voting and counting, called alternate voting (AV) or ranked-choice voting, is an objectively better approach than FPTP. It also solves some problems that come with the winner-takes-all system: it's easily possible in the FPTP system for extreme bigotry that inflames the passions of a committed minority to win multi-cornered contests. The AV method makes that more difficult, as candidates need broad-based acceptance to win. In that sense, AV forces moderation upon candidates.

A combination of PR and AV may mitigate the worst effects of FPTP. For instance, we could design a parliament by tweaking the AV logic to elect the two most acceptable candidates in every constituency. This could well be done by picking the top two candidates in an RC system. The new system would then have two MPs elected from the same constituency (who may both have lost in an FPTP race). The extent to which a committed minority can corrupt public choice is a serious threat to democracy, and one that's perpetuated by FPTP. A combination of AV and PR could help solve that.

A Problem Without a Solution

Whatever the voting method and election mechanism in the representative model, this model itself is problematic in a basic sense. That is, in all its methods, voters will still have too many contradicting policy positions for any one representative, or a selected few, to represent. The total number of permutations of all the positions of all voters in a constituency is easily far greater than all the atoms in the universe. That is a truth. Therefore, no electoral system in the world can seek a perfectly faithful representation of the people's will through the representative model either – least of all through FPTP.

The representative model's inability to accurately reflect the will of the people on all issues is discounted as the price to pay for the ease of functioning and the stability of government. It is, after all, a better reflection of the will of the people than absolute monarchy. It introduces a controlled diversity of opinion in policymaking, which gives people the impression that they can influence the laws that govern them even though their ability to influence any given law is negligible.

There is an additional complicating factor: a single individual representing a couple of million citizens was not something people could have conceived of in the late middle ages when the Westminster system evolved in England. It is probable that the total number of eligible voters across all constituencies for the English Parliament were less than that of a single constituency in present-day India.

The problem of scale in the current Indian context makes the issue many orders of magnitude more problematic. A typical constituency in the Indo-Gangetic plains has about 1.5 million eligible voters. A back-of-the-envelope calculation suggests the probability of impact of each vote in a relatively close bipolar race using FPTP is e^{-424}, an absurdly small probability, which often makes one wonder why anyone bothers to vote. And here we have simplified the problem. In reality, there are multiple policy positions, and every voter will have opinions and policy positions that do not align neatly with those of the candidates. The probability, therefore, of a voter's ability to impact a specific policy decision through the lever of voting for a representative is so low that it is 0 for all practical purposes.

What would a rational citizen in such a system do?

Kenneth Arrow famously came up with a theorem that says there is no way to design a fair mechanism of electing candidates reflecting the will of the people. It defines three reasonable conditions of fairness:

- If every voter prefers alternative X over alternative Y, then the group prefers X over Y.
- If every voter's preference between X and Y remains unchanged, then the group's preference between X and Y will also remain unchanged (even if voters' preferences between other pairs like X and Z, Y and Z, or Z and W change).
- There is no 'dictator': no single voter possesses the power to always determine the group's preference.

Arrow states that no electoral system can satisfy all these three conditions. This extends not just to election of political representatives but equally to any social choices that a group of individuals makes using voting mechanisms of any kind. It's an important theorem, if only to understand that all electoral mechanisms are flawed and the reason for choosing a voting system is because it is least flawed – like democracy itself.

The mathematical reality of elections in a representative

democracy, therefore, is: we elect representatives with votes that have a very, very, low probability of impact. That vote to choose the representative then translating into a vote for a policy preference has a probability of impact that's practically 0. And, on top of that, there's no way to pick either a candidate or a policy in a perfectly fair way, whatever the mode of election.

A reasonable design criterion in such a scenario would be to reduce the number of layers between the electorate and the end objective – governing policies that they voted for – to an absolute minimum. The concept of MPs voting on our behalf in Parliament, for instance, suffers the same problem as our choosing them in the first place. They vote often, though; their votes on bills are usually passed by a simple majority too. This means, each time they vote they are transmitting the choice of their electors, for which they are imperfect transmitters.

Secondly, their votes suffer from the limitations of Arrow's Impossibility Theorem as well. Each Bill passed, each vote of confidence undertaken and each budget allocation voted on is a layer that introduces a new error factor and, therefore, corrupts the original choice a little more. This predicament, in theory, is not unique to India, but the size and scale of the country magnify it to proportions unseen anywhere else. No other country has a single MP representing over 2 million citizens, and therefore no other country has a situation where each voter has such a low probability of impact on outcomes. These two factors – a single representative for a constituency the size of a small European country, and each voter having practically zero impact on governance – together make the system akin to oligarchy and less like a representative democracy.

There are a couple of additional constraints placed on elected MPs in India that render them utterly ineffective as representatives of their constituencies: the party whip and the anti-defection law. Individual MPs in India are bound by law to their party in terms of their vote inside Parliament; and the only way they can choose to vote otherwise is if they formally split away from their party, for which they need a third of all elected members belonging to that party. This abstraction of power away from the elected MP to the party leadership is another layer that debases the original choice of the voter. That is, even if there's a magically perfect alignment between an elected representative and her electorate, and even if the limitations of Arrow's Theorem did not apply, the representative still cannot vote as she pleases. She can only vote the way her party tells her to.

Voting mechanisms inside Parliament can be seen as an unfair system that is a distilled version of the one outside. It suffers from all the flaws of the basic electoral system that elects representatives. And this system is used several hundreds of times in a given parliamentary term, amplifying those flaws each time. If at all one wanted to fix the electoral system, one could begin from inside Parliament, therefore. It's a closed universe with smaller numbers. This is easier to grapple with. And in Parliament the transmission problem is so acute that it is obvious even to those who do not think India has a problem with the way its democracy is implemented.

MPs in Parliament have no ability to vote on issues based on what their conscience tells them or what their constituents tell them. They have to vote based on what their party bosses tell them.

In many other countries, there are rebel MPs who don't vote with their party on specific issues. But even in those systems where MPs can vote their conscience in theory, very few do so in practice. It is detrimental to the careers of individual politicians if they don't toe the party line. An MP who doesn't toe the party line is likely to lose his ability to become a minister or land other sought-after appointments. Politicians, like the rest of us, respond to career incentives. And political parties control the career ladder.

An obvious question that could be asked now is: why can't we let MPs use a secret ballot, like the voters who elect them? That would work to eliminate the power that party bosses accrue to themselves; but that would also mean MPs can't be held accountable, either by their constituents or by their parties, given that their votes are now secret. An absence of such transparency results in an absence of accountability, which is crucial for representative democracy.

Political parties and governments would have another problem with such a system because they would never be sure if their government will survive. No government can function in such an uncertain environment.

A second option would be a hybrid of these two approaches. Analogous to combining AV and PR, MPs could be allowed to cast a certain percentage of all their votes in a secret ballot. This will enable MPs wanting cover from their party bosses to hide some of their votes – especially those made against the party line.

There are problems with this too, however. First of all, party bosses would get an inkling of who the likely rebels are by simply looking at which votes the MPs opted to keep secret. Second, if a bill fails, and the rest of the votes are transparent, it is easy to figure out how those voting in secret cast their ballots.

Whatever clever method one can come up with for MPs to vote in Parliaments, it would be a trade-off between accountability, stability and honest representation of the people's will. In this trade-off, the factor most easily sacrificed is representation of the people's will. It's an abstract idea that is easy to discount, given that MPs are elected by people in the first place. While this problem exists in all countries that follow the Westminster model, India has further vitiated the problem with laws on anti-defection, which act over and above the natural complication from scale.

The quirk of relegating representation and transmission of the people's will to an afterthought is not unexpected. Representative democracy in the Westminster model owes its origin to the way the Parliament of England evolved in the period between its securing the Magna Carta (1215) and the English Civil Wars (1642–51).

That model had Barons or tenants-in-chief as the first MPs. It is a model that represents the interests of the Barons as a counter to those of the monarch; any benefits of representation the people may have had in such a system were a side-effect.

Modern liberal democracies have surely come a long way from those medieval times; but the structure of Parliament still retains vestiges of the earlier system in terms of transmission inefficiencies. Sometimes it seems as if we have exchanged Barons for elected MPs. If the modern party bosses controlling MPs and policy choices look and feel like feudal lords and the fiefdoms they guard, respectively, it's partly by design.

Political parties and party bosses seeking to centralize decisions are behaving, in some ways, like the overall system they belong to: they concentrate power at the party level so that the party votes and acts in unison to secure stability and achieve results for itself. The government and Parliament act in exactly the same manner too.

Every single player in this system is acting this way, including individual legislators seeking to move up in their career. But, given that these players are engaged in this struggle for accruing power and achieving results within their term in Parliament, they often ignore the question of long-term structural stability. That stability is often inversely related to the degree to which power is centralized. That is, a system where power is centralized in the hands of a few players is not stable in the long term. It is considered axiomatic by political scientists that a system with multiple points of veto takes a longer time to achieve results, but it achieves results that are more stable.

In a multiparty federal structure, individual MPs, the parties they belong to in Parliament and the states with their own set of legislators, who in turn belong to different parties, are the various 'vetoes'. This system working well would mean a low chance of any nationwide, sweeping legislation-passing, which would be a slow process as well. But once any legislation is passed, there would be stability, given that its undoing will be just as difficult. The probability of achieving two rare events back to back being even rarer is the simple arithmetical reality that yields this stability.

In recent times, though, the Indian Parliament has rushed controversial legislation through, using questionable procedural means despite significant opposition. Not only does this centralizing of power lead to unstable outcomes, but it also ends up encouraging short-term thinking among politicians. If MPs are not sure what they are doing is going to stand the test of time, they'll naturally focus on doing things for the short term that may help them get re-elected.

This is a particularly dangerous situation, given that the biggest policy challenge of the twenty-first century is the combating of climate change, which will be a decades-long process impacting future generations. This demands sacrifices today so that generations that are not born yet can live fulfilling lives. It is exactly the kind of policy problem that the current system will fail miserably to tackle.

In effect, in the model of democracy spawned by the Magna Carta, we elect an individual and not a policy, for historical reasons. The representative we elect cannot represent us perfectly because that is theoretically impossible. Even if they wish to represent us reasonably, and not perfectly, the Indian Parliament imposes restrictions on how they can vote, and this makes the model unviable.

We also use election mechanisms that result in candidate choices that aren't true reflections of people's choices. The result of all this is that we have a polity that's a poor representation of the people's will, and politicians who are disincentivized to think long term or look beyond bettering their own careers and, therefore, inclined to seek power for its own sake. This system resembles an efficient oligarchy when it is functioning well, and regresses into feudalism when things break down.

Many suggestions have been made over time to improve the existing model of democracy. One ancient idea that has been rediscovered in recent times is sortition. That is, instead of electing MPs, we could randomly pick a citizen through a lottery to represent a constituency.

This circumvents the systemic biases of our electoral system to some extent and dismantles the political party infrastructure as a power base. Individual MPs who don't belong to a party do not have to follow the rules of anti-defection or a party whip. And because they are chosen at random, vested interests cannot possibly prop them up by funding their candidature. Elite capture of entire political parties is also ruled out.

Sortition, however, merely solves the quirks of electoral democracy in the representative mould that electoral democracy in the representative mould itself has introduced. It doesn't solve the basic problem of representation being an inefficient method of transmitting the people's will. Worse, it doesn't attempt to transmit the people's will, even if inefficiently. That makes any organizing to effect social change impossible. It also destroys expertise in policymaking, which is already in short supply. Sortition, by itself, throws the baby (democratic principles) out with the bathwater (inefficient transmission). Can we combine this with other methods to achieve the results we seek?

2

The Athenian Model

India's Problem Thus Far

India has a Magna Carta version of representative democracy that poorly transmits the will of the people. This democratic model is situated in a federal structure that is skewed towards a powerful Union, where the Centre tends to accrue ever greater power at the expense of states' rights.

Such a unitary approach to governance, in a diverse country with various states at varying stages of development, renders most nationwide policies suboptimal for most states and, therefore, for most people. This centralized approach, owing to its skewed structure, has already forced states into a zero-sum game when it comes to resource allocation.

The sharing of revenue and other pooled resources in such a complicated environment ends up with perverse outcomes and incentives such as encouragement of population growth. These problems cannot be resolved satisfactorily within the

The Athenian Model

contours of the current structure. Further, this system risks tyranny by investing extraordinary powers in the hands of individual leaders and party bosses, in effect making most of the elected MPs powerless.

Thus, the status quo works only for those elected to office in the Union government as they accrue greater power for themselves and cement their positions, while achieving poor outcomes for everyone else and all other entities. Such a government sacrifices democracy's major advantage – that of creating a slow-moving equilibrium that tends to progress peacefully towards better solutions with time as society evolves – at the altar of those few who can choose between being oligarchs or tyrants.

Most democracies around the world do use some version of what we have called the Magna Carta model, where representatives are elected from a specific geography and who then vote on that geography's behalf in Parliament to make laws. This works reasonably in some cases, where the populations are small and relatively homogeneous. It tends to be a particularly poor fit for large and diverse federations like India for all the reasons discussed in the previous chapters.

A natural contrast to this model of democracy, should we need to think of one, is the Athenian version of democracy. In this, instead of using representatives as a tool to transmit our choices, the people directly make decisions.

Direct Democracy

The Athenian model was a system of government that made Athens a stable and prosperous city state in the ancient world. From the fifth century BCE to the third century BCE, Athens was what we'd now call a direct democracy. It wasn't the only city state that practised such a system, but it sure was the largest that did so, and a model for self-governing city states across the Mediterranean.

Ancient Athens did not merely inspire its contemporaries. The American and French Revolutions in the late eighteenth century, which both contributed substantially to the modern liberal order as we know it, had their main actors claim inspiration from the Athenian model. The best definition of this version of democracy is often attributed to Pericles, who in a speech at an Athenian funeral is supposed to have said:

> It has the name democracy because the government is in the hands not of the few but of the majority. In private disputes all are equal before the law; and when it comes to esteem in public affairs, a man is preferred according to his own reputation for something, not, on the whole, just turn and turn about, but for excellence, and even in poverty no man is debarred by obscurity of reputation so long as he has it in him to do some good service to the State. Freedom is a feature of our public life; and as for suspicion of one another in our daily private pursuits, we do not frown on our neighbour if he behaves to please

himself or set our faces in those expressions of disapproval that are so disagreeable, however harmless.[1]

Athens, the largest known city state in the world back then, decided all matters of public importance by discussion amongst citizens in an assembly. More than a voting mechanism, it was a method by which citizens – albeit only free men (not women or slaves) – tried to convince each other about their points of view through logical argument and arrive at a consensus. They made decisions on public policy, budgeting, war and peace; they also acted as courts of justice. The transmission efficiency of the people's will, a vexing issue in representative models, one can imagine, would have been quite high.

Platonic Ideals and Government

The Athenian version of democracy, though, ended up as a pejorative by late antiquity. The city state of Athens, after all, convicted its most famous citizen, Socrates, and sentenced him to death by poison. His crime was to have encouraged among young people what we'd now call a scientific temper.

Socrates's student Plato, whose discourse on government, *The Republic*, is still considered the seminal treatise on the subject, wasn't a fan of democracy. *The Republic* considers democracy as a sign of decay that is one step removed from tyranny. It famously picks aristocracy as the ideal form of government. It imagines a philosopher king who'd value wisdom and reason over material pursuits. Such a ruler comes from an aristocratic ruling class, which is similarly highly educated and does not seek power or wealth for itself. This utopian aristocrat seeks the metaphysical good, which the Platonic ideal envisions as the ultimate good of which all other forms of good – such as happiness – are mere shadows.

He (and it's usually a he), does not own property or seek to enhance his own wealth or that of his citizens. Instead, ordinary citizens, who are allowed to own property, sustain the beneficent aristocrats by the material wealth they generate. This scheme imagines society as having three distinct classes: the aristocratic ruling class, the military class and common folk. While the qualifying criterion for getting into the aristocratic class is education and embodiment of the Platonic ideal, to a reader from the Indian subcontinent it is suspiciously reminiscent of the caste order.

The Platonic view of government ranks aristocracy – with a philosopher king at its helm – above timocracy, oligarchy, democracy and tyranny, this ranking order being the road map of decay from the ideal of aristocracy. The children of enlightened aristocrats, we are warned, can fall ever so slightly from the Platonic ideal and allow wealth generation to become a part of governing. This corruption of the aristocrat's soul isn't a corruption of the aristocrat himself but of the governing structure, if not the philosophy. *The Republic* calls such a system 'timocracy'. The problem with timocracy is not that it is bad in terms of its governing outcomes – except maybe that the ruler isn't standing up for the enlightened ideal. The real problem, it would appear, is that its decay into oligarchy is inevitable, according to Plato.

The explicit decay of timocracy into a system where the ruling class seeks wealth for itself, that being a corruption of both the structure and philosophy of governance, is what Plato calls oligarchy. That is, those in power seek to enhance their personal wealth through the levers of public policy. A further decay of oligarchy to not even allow for moderation – another crucial Platonic ideal, which the oligarchs apparently retain even if it is for their narrow self-interest – is how we end up with democracy, according to *The Republic*.

The democratic man in this worldview is one who is incapable of distinguishing the necessary from what can be resisted. He seeks freedom for the self above the Platonic ideals of rationalism and wisdom; these men aggregate to the unthinking teeming masses, and if they are allowed to take control it results in majoritarian anarchy. A tyrant then emerges in the form of a saviour to save the people from their own self-inflicted anarchy. This, Plato imagines, would be the logical next step in a society where ordinary citizens prize freedom and material wealth – except that they eventually surrender both their freedom and wealth to the tyrant.

These ideas, especially the concept that common citizens should subjugate themselves to an aristocracy in order to achieve a perfect government, is unpalatable in the post-French-Revolution world. Equality of citizens is now a goal in itself. That this may mean people will seek to achieve their personal desires over and above a considered civilizational good is something we take for granted. Regardless, we should give no one person, or any single class, the right to decide what's a civilizational good.

The individualism of our modern approach, however, is exactly what makes the Platonic fear – loss of moderation – come true. That is, individual participants will seek to achieve their personal desires through public policy; or, at best, influence public policy towards what they think is in the best public interest in their lay view. This, in all likelihood, won't be as good as that of a sophisticated philosopher king's view. This idea of individuals seeking what is in their best interests is antithetical to the Platonic ideal, exactly because the individual doesn't trust the masses, or Demos, to ever act in ways that are aligned towards achieving the Platonic ideal.

However, in the modern context we have seen that the lay view and the aggregation of it to run society is both more just than other systems and in practice yields the best results. This is just because we do not like the concept of a king, philosopher or otherwise, or an aristocratic elite. We imagine a society in which all individuals are created equal, or at least have equal rights.

Also, we have come to understand that the wisdom of crowds generates better outcomes over the long term in matters that aren't an exact science. It is counterintuitive, but crowdsourcing beats experts, be they philosopher kings or overpaid fund managers, almost every time. We have built society assuming this wisdom of crowds to be axiomatic. The entire modern financial system, for example, runs on some version of this.

Even if the wisdom of crowds doesn't yield perfect results, we'd still settle for a system where we do not have a philosopher king. We now think of imperfect results as a problem worth having, even if the solutions to sidestep them aren't easy or elegant. And, unlike Plato, we do not hold on to the purity of metaphysical good as our goal. We'd like our governments, instead, to be a reasonable reflection of who we are as a people. If that reflection ends up as less than ideal, it's up to us to change ourselves.

The caveat to this, of course, is that the overall system remains stable while we try and improve ourselves in order to improve the reflection. We certainly want to make sure society doesn't descend into anarchy and tyranny, as Plato warns us it would, in the time it takes for us to organically improve society. In doing this, we are in fact seeking a Platonic ideal: moderation at the heart of systems design for society.

One of the problems that's often a point of serious contention in democratic societies is: what do we do with new or existing laws that are unfair or unjust? For example, what happens when there are racist, sexist, casteist or other illiberal laws on the books? Or, if the new laws enacted happen to be antithetical to liberalism? Do we throw them out because one group seeks that, holding that those laws are unfair? Who decides what's unfair? And, giving a perfectly well-meaning liberal elite that power, or even merely the power to frame that question as such, results in a backlash that's familiar to us as culture-war politics.

Ordinary people often take up reactionary positions to assert their equality vis-à-vis the liberal elite in such a dogfight. They may not even care deeply for the positions they fight for, but they are in it to win it as a tribe. Non-cooperation of this kind can get particularly vicious in a representative democracy where politicians have an incentive to encourage such cleavages in society. Over and above the basic problem of their poor transmission efficiency, representative models, with their incentive structures for individuals, can poison people's ability to trust society.

Even if these problems of poor incentives and bad-faith actors in society did not exist, the core problem still remains. That is, the morality of a population at a given point may not be in step with the best understanding of moral philosophy at that point. All democratic systems have to face up to this conundrum and try to find solutions.

The Athenians approached this by putting each issue to a popular vote. Plato wanted error to be on the side of the philosopher king's enlightened judgement. Modern representative democracies yield to elected representatives who happen to be career politicians. Often, those politicians imagine themselves to be philosopher kings while having to face the reality of populist pressures during elections. It is designed to be the best of both worlds; it often ends up as the worst of both worlds.

The various permutations between these options offer an

interesting exercise in trade-offs. But whatever the system, a basic truth of a well-functioning democracy is that it can't have laws that are completely out of step with the sensibilities of its people. Having a philosopher king, or for that matter a representative who is an enlightened liberal, in what is a deeply bigoted society, is no solution. What we would want is a system that fairly reflects the will of the people while preventing the most egregious bigotry.

Plato's worry wasn't merely that democracy would legitimate people valuing their own freedoms over the metaphysical good. His concern was that such a population was at risk of being trapped into tyranny. In his time, that risk was one step removed; that is, the tyrant would replace an existing direct democracy as an entire system of governance.

In modern electoral democracies that follow a representative model, the tyranny is a lot less explicit and, therefore, more insidious. Representative models allow a gradual accrual of power in the hands of the executive. Worse, they legitimize that accrual of power by way of narrative-building in political campaigns and communication.

A problem with the representative model is that it has a tendency to reduce politics to a cult of personality. The presidential campaigns of the United States are probably the world's most outlandish examples of this. But elections in most other democracies of relatively large countries, even those using the Westminster system where voters don't elect the executive directly, routinely get reduced to a popularity contest among the candidates as opposed to a policy choice.

This systemic bug even passes for a feature when one's preferred cult wins.

The obvious flaw of politics of personality is that no human is flawless. Democracies acknowledge that and offer a system of institutional checks and balances as a solution. However, as recent happenings have demonstrated repeatedly across multiple countries, those institutions can fail under the weight of a charismatic populist. Having such a leader runs counter to the raison d'être of democracy even, in that we do not want a king or a 'great man' to embody the republic. The great man theory of politics and history is as untenable to the modern sensibility as having a philosopher king. The representative model of democracy, which does exactly that, somehow manages to squeak through because we have periodic elections.

Not only does the 'great man theory'-infused view of politics make the entire set-up ripe for capture by a charismatic populist in troubled times, it often paves the way for a vicious cycle. That is, it generates an environment where great men are highly in demand at the expense of policy. Politicians who offer their personal virtue as a solution demonize other politicians by definition, thus vitiating the political atmosphere. Increasing the insecurities of the political class only incentivizes all of them to seek greater power for themselves at the expense of civil liberties, which get eroded, and policy outcomes, which turn out suboptimal. Anti-corruption campaigns as propaganda are a prime example of this. That corruption among those in power is a basic human flaw that anyone can fall prey to is lost in the populist battle. A change of personnel is never a solution to corruption; yet that's exactly what the charismatic offer.

Even when they function at high efficiency, political parties can be problematic. They are often turned into vehicles of personal ambition in such an environment. Andrew Wyatt, in his book *Party System Change in South India: Political Entrepreneurs, Patterns and Processes*, calls these politicians entrepreneurs, and charts the formation of political parties that closely resemble business enterprises. These parties, for example, often do not have an ideologically inclined cadre. They do not have bench strength; and their decision-makers are often a coterie.

Can we imagine a solution that avoids these obvious traps of both the Athenian model and the modern representative model and yet retains their foundational principles? That will be explored in the next chapter.

3

An Alternative

Gamified Direct Democracy

One obvious and simplistic solution to the problems of current-day democracy and its poor transmission efficiency is to move closer to the Athenian model. But that solution can be worse than the problem it seeks to solve. So, the question now is, how do we design a system that transmits the will of the people better but retains the current guard rails – such as institutionalized checks and balances that aim for moderation – or improves upon them?

The idea of the Athenian model isn't entirely unheard of in the modern world. Several countries, for example, use ballot initiatives at different levels of government. These have varying degrees of power and influence in the way they are implemented in each country.

For example, in the United States, several states have ballot initiatives that allow citizens to vote on specific questions. Italy and Switzerland, on the other hand, have a more prominent role for referendums at the national level. The Constitution of Italy uses direct democracy to allow its citizens to reject existing laws using a popular vote of citizens; people can seek a referendum on any amendment made to the Constitution and can pass non-binding advisory that legislative bodies can then take up.

The legislative branches of government in these systems, however, accrue enough power to sidestep the referendum pressures to a large degree. Even if they don't, it's by design that the elected representatives, through the legislature, are more powerful in all these systems where referendums are an option.

A true move towards a modern version of the Athenian model would be a referendum process that cannot be subsumed by the elected legislature. It would give direct democracy powers to the people, independent of the representative model. For example, the simplest and likely most simplistic option would be to disband the powers of elected representatives to make laws and allow a direct referendum process to do that.

This has the obvious advantage of improving transmission efficiency. That is, people can vote directly on the laws that govern them instead of electing a representative who then votes on their behalf to enact laws. Not only is this option better at transmitting the people's will, it also eliminates the party structures and other distortions that come in the way of the people's will. The problems with such a system are also obvious: the threat of it sliding into majoritarian tyranny, the loss of expertise in lawmaking that exists in institutions such as Parliament, the lack of oversight that Joint Parliamentary Committees can perform and, finally, the loss of an intangible aspect that we call political leadership.

The common criticism of direct democracy – that it is a short slide away from majoritarian tyranny – is well founded but also overwrought. The history of the world, particularly in the twentieth century, is littered with genocides that had popular support. Being wary of any system that could allow the majority in any society to legitimize extreme violence comes from a reasonable fear.

The evidence from existing societies with referendums is that the laws passed through such a system are not significantly more anti-minority or significantly more skewed towards conservatism than laws passed by elected legislatures. But that is hardly a point of comfort when people fear the worst in moments of crises. A systemic solution to address such a fear will have to be in place as an a priori condition for any change to even be considered.

Majoritarian tyranny that may hurt minorities is closely linked to another criticism of direct democracy – that it discards expertise for populism. This is a fair objection, given the history of populist movements. Populist groupthink not only discards expertise, it often also seeks to pin blame on experts and relegate them to the status of minorities. Fascist and tyrannical movements are often characterized by such populism as a necessary condition. A system that seeks to replace an existing representative democracy with direct democracy, thus, should seek to isolate expertise and the evaluations by that expertise from the passions of the moment, however inflamed those might be.

Incorporating both aspects – genuine expertise and legitimate popular will – and retaining them as independent channels of input for policymaking will be a challenge for any society. To achieve that systemically should be a goal for any system seeking to replace the existing order.

In the 1980s, several local governments in Brazil started adopting participatory budget making – that is, they allowed citizens a direct say in the municipal budget. This grew in popularity and has now been adopted in many cities in Asia, Africa and Europe. However, this form of direct democracy is extremely limited in its scope, and cities that adopted them still have a significant skew towards representatives.

An improvement upon both this model and sortition (which we mentioned earlier) is the Ostbelgien Model of east Belgium. This model, adopted since 2019, divorces authority to propose something for a vote from the actual vote. The power to bring a piece of legislation to a vote is held by a body that is chosen by sortition, while the actual vote on the proposal is cast by an elected parliament.

This achieves the purpose of saving the legislative process from hyperpartisanship; the legislative calendar, which is otherwise controlled by party bosses, often falls prey to the politics of the day. The Ostbelgien Model insulates in some ways the power to seek change from the power to effect change, thereby acting as a cooling chamber of sorts. It could also have the effect of reflecting the long-term interests in policymaking that elected politicians with pressures to deliver in the short term often ignore. However, legislators still belong to political parties and their transmission efficiency is still poor under this system.

The Ostbelgien Model, in effect, adds a useful layer of veto but doesn't solve the underlying problem of transmission inefficiency. We can easily imagine an improvement, though. We could retain the independent body that has the power to decide the legislative timetable. Its members could well be chosen by sortition; that is a method which works well for choosing a small group that has power over process but not outcome. We could even add another body or panel that's chosen for its expertise on drafting legislation. This additional body could also be picked by sortition, albeit with some gatekeeping conditions for maintaining its purpose as an expert panel of sorts.

The actual vote, though, the one that elected legislators cast in the original Ostbelgien Model, can then be made a direct vote. It would be a vote which people cast, not their representatives. Thus, the power to select something for a vote rests with a small group elected by sortition; the power to draft that particular piece of legislation rests with another group of experts similarly picked by sortition; the power to say yes or no to that proposal rests with the people.

While the power to bring something to vote and the power to draft legislation are important steps in themselves, a more pressing question in a democracy is often about what should be brought in as a legislative proposal at all. That power, one can imagine, rests with the people, as it does in many systems where referenda are allowed. This has relevance to improved transmission efficiency under direct democracy. A practical implementation of it, though, would be one where routine affairs of the government, such as budgeting to run the government and other basic executive actions that are compliant with existing laws, are brought in by a separate council of the executive branch of government.

Any new legislation that isn't routine government business, however, could only be introduced by the voters themselves. And all proposals – whether for routine government business or for a fundamental change in the way society is run – would be voted on by the people. The difference, though, could be that while the former doesn't have any turnout thresholds to pass, the latter does.

The above system offers a three-legged stool: it transmits the will of the people better; it allows for deliberation and moderation by giving the power of bringing something to a vote to a body that isn't beholden to political passions of the day; and it incorporates expertise in the form of a drafting committee.

However, the perennial question that has plagued any and all direct-democracy proposals – that of majoritarian triumphalism taking hold – needs specific systemic solutions to convince the people, particularly minorities and those who've been historically marginalized, that such a system will not descend into what they fear. Granting a body that's selected by sortition the power to decide the legislative timetable is one way to insulate such a direct democracy from the politics of the moment.

But there's no reason to believe that those who are selected thus will not be swayed by life around them. After all, if sortition works as it is intended to, the median feeling in a body selected by some random process on any issue will reflect that of the population at large. And, more importantly, that body's purpose is to bring about moderation by acting as a cooling chamber; it's no solution to possible venality in society.

Our goal is: We want a democratic system that functions well and is considered satisfactory by citizens. This must not only transmit the will of the people without compromising on expertise and without falling prey to short-termism, it must also render the majoritarian capture of government near impossible.

The design criteria that satisfy these constraints are those that assume the best intentions of the people over the long arc of history but restrain them from moving quickly. Even if there are illiberal impulses in the collective conscience of society, the system should restrain their ability to inflict too much damage in a short span of time, in the hope that better sense will prevail over time. The price to pay for that, naturally, is that society's ability to move forward – even on what we may consider its best ideas – is limited by the same sense of moderation and caution. In other words, the system should be conservative in design but liberal in its goals, regardless of the politics of the day.

To achieve that, consider the following system: Imagine the basic structure as the improved Ostbelgien Model discussed above. That is, we have two panels, chosen by sortition, that decide on the timing and drafting of legislation, respectively. The bills themselves are voted on by citizens with a yes or no, after being carefully drafted by a separate committee.

To start with, let's assume each citizen will be given a fixed number of votes, say N. One could fix N as the moving average of 10 per cent of the total number of bills passed each year for the last ten years. The reason for limiting the number of votes to 10 per cent of the total bills passed is so that people consider their vote a potent weapon to be used sparingly and strategically. That would be in keeping with conservative systems design and will become more apparent when we understand the ways in which these votes can be used.

Citizens can use the N votes they initially get in two distinct ways:

- Be a signatory voter who seeks a new piece of legislation. This is a stage that can be thought of as a legislative request by citizens. To bring up a legislation for consideration by the drafting panel, it would need, say, at least 20 per cent of all eligible voters to sign on/vote at this stage. And if a citizen signs on at this stage, and the proposal does get the requisite 20 per cent to take it to the next stage, the total votes hold by the citizen now number N-1. That is, the citizen has spent one vote to successfully bring a piece of legislation for consideration. On the other hand, if this proposal does not get the requisite 20 per cent support, that citizen's total remaining votes are restored to what they were earlier. That is, a citizen isn't punished for wanting something that did not happen.

- Be a voter in the general referendum. This general referendum is for bills/legislative proposals that are brought to a vote by the panel that decides when to schedule such referenda after the drafting panel has fixed the exact language and content of the legislation. Voters who support the legislation can vote for it, and those who don't will vote against it. We can set a reasonable threshold of at least 40 per cent turnout, for example, to make the vote valid. If a voter votes yes in this referendum and if that referendum effort wins by a simple majority, it becomes law. And those voters who voted yes to create this new law will see their total remaining votes decrease by one each. However, if they voted yes and the referendum did not pass, their vote count would be restored to what it was before they cast their vote.

For proposals introduced by the executive branch that are business as usual and required to maintain the status quo, the turnout condition and threshold requirement could be eliminated.

Importantly, voters who want to vote against any bill in a referendum will not see their remainder vote count change, *regardless of the outcome*. That is, the system will not punish a voter if some legislation they did not want is passed. Nor will it punish those who seek the statusquo.

While a voter can use only one vote to vote in favour of a new law, we could add an 'all-in' clause for a veto. Let a voter use all their remaining votes to vote no to a new bill to prevent a new law from coming into being. And, since they are voting no, those votes will remain with them regardless of passage or failure of the law.

This system is generous to citizens in encouraging them to seek change. But its design is very conservative and calls for a large consensus to actually effect any serious legislative change. More importantly, people are empowered to resist change more easily than effect change.

In practice, if some fringe majoritarian group wants to bring in a law that is seriously problematic to a minority group, it will be an uphill climb to pass such a majoritarian piece of legislation. That is, the group needs to first convince 20 per cent of the electorate to spend a vote to bring it up for consideration. Then that proposal has to pass through two panels elected by sortition. Finally, the fringe needs to convince the general population that the proposed law is so important that they get a large turnout with people prepared to spend one of their votes for their fringe cause.

Almost everyone from the majority community may need to turn out in the above example of fringe legislation, because if some section of the population thinks the proposed legislation is illiberal or unfair towards them, they could all use all their N votes at once, thereby achieving a veto. This veto power, because it's a no vote, does not end with a single use. The minority gets a veto as long as enough of them disagree and have enough votes left over to use up for a veto, over and above the majority's one-vote-per-person effort.

That is, the system allows the minority vote to become orders of magnitude more potent than their population when it comes to vetoes. This system, one can safely conclude, has far stronger guard rails than the existing methods of lawmaking in terms of avoiding majoritarian tyranny.

The price to pay for such a system is, of course, that progress, even in areas of broad consensus, will take time and not be easy. It is a fair price any system that seeks stability will have to pay. While the advantage of such a model is that it would be a true representation of the people's will without the threat of a majoritarian march, the criticism against it could well be that the status quo is already stacked against some minorities and that needs radical change. Perhaps the hope is that the will of the people will bend towards a liberal, just and verdant society over time. The alternatives could be either unstable radicalism or tyrannical majoritarianism.

This is a thought experiment, of course. Parliament and state legislatures, which are all stuffed with career politicians focused on furthering their own careers, would have to opt for replacing themselves and handing over power under such a structure.

But let's imagine that Mandrake the Magician made one of his powerful hypnotic gestures and convinced them to quit. Could this sort of direct democracy solve many of India's seemingly intractable problems?

It would magically solve the transmission problem entirely. It would also resolve the problem of votes being weighted differently. A voter in Uttar Pradesh will now have as much weightage as a voter in Tamil Nadu.

Punishing Tamil Nadu for policy success, or punishing the citizens of Uttar Pradesh for what is a governance failure, will not arise under this system. Both sets of citizens also get to have a powerful veto.

The other impossibly knotty issue of Indian states being entangled in a zero-sum game when it comes to resource allocation may also be relatively easier to deal with. States like Tamil Nadu and Kerala will behave like minority voters and consistently thwart any centralizing policy moves that tend towards input parameters as the metrics to track; similarly, states in the Indo-Gangetic plains will thwart centralizing ideas that veer towards output metrics.

Any legislation that has varying impact across states will fail at the federal level. This, it's hoped, will ensure that the federal structure devolves power naturally to decentralized, self-governing states and retains only the absolute minimum necessary powers. Not only will states then have a permanent veto vis-à-vis the Union, but local governments (panchayats and municipalities) will also have a veto vis-à-vis the states as this model is extended to local governments.

This model of gamified direct democracy offers a broad three-legged stool for a stable, just and continuously evolving society. India, in practice, would then resemble the European Union in terms of its federal structure and compare more closely with the city states of antiquity in terms of its local governments. As the voting pool expands for national-level votes, the possibilities of veto expand and therefore there are likely to be fewer legislative changes at the Centre.

India as a Gamified Direct Democracy

It's useful to imagine such a system and conjecture how it might work in practice to solve or mitigate India's seemingly intractable problems.

Let's assume we had the same system of government – in terms of law enforcement, bureaucracy, judiciary, et al. – we now have, and only the lawmaking bodies of Parliament, state legislatures and local governments were replaced with the system of gamified direct democracy proposed above.

Such a system would strengthen the localized idea of 'my society'. After all, most people care for their immediate lives a lot more than issues that affect distant lands.

Voters are also likely to use the power of veto for tangible issues that affect their lives directly.

If an abstract idea or events in a distant land play a big factor in their votes, it has to come from the ground up and can't be imposed top down in such a system. This eliminates or greatly reduces certain perverse incentives. It would also be hard to weaponize abstractions such as nationalism, which cause such inflammatory rhetoric under the current system.

For starters, consider the budget. There are centrally sponsored flagship schemes that amount to Rs 3.81 lakh crore. These are schemes that typically impose centrally conceived programmes on states. If the budget needs to be passed using the method above, these schemes will simply not be passed.

Much of the expenditure in the Union budget addresses state subjects with policies and solutions that are suboptimal for most states. Since our direct voting system would stop usurpation of states' rights on the expenditure side, revenue collection will also shrink correspondingly over time.

The Indian Union is skewed towards the Centre primarily through the power of taxation; most, or one could argue all, of its other powers stem from the power of the purse. What the new structure will do, slowly and over time, is remove that skew by taking the purse away. This will hopefully allow states and local governments to assume what is rightfully their responsibility. These local bodies would also have the power to tax their own citizens locally for the newly assumed functions, since the power of the referendum will allow them to place such schemes to the vote.

Consider contentious legislation that has been passed in haste during the tenure of the 16h and 17th Lok Sabhas. This includes GST, the three Farm Laws, the unilateral dissolution of Jammu & Kashmir's statehood and amendments to the Citizenship Act.

These laws most likely wouldn't have passed the two-stage process described above. They'd all likely have failed at the first stage. If they somehow managed to pass that, they'd have been cooled down by the panels that decide their drafting and timing. And if they magically did pass these barriers too, they likely would have been rejected by a vocal minority that considers them a threat to their basic life and liberty. And if, somehow, the majority were so unanimous and persistent in seeking to implement their writ on these varied minorities – ranging from farmers in Punjab, to ordinary Kashmiris, to protesting Assamese – they'd have to sacrifice a significant portion of their political capital and risk ceding future control under the new voting mechanism.

Consider the intractable problem of allocation ratios for tax devolution from the previous chapters. Seen as a single, centralized problem to solve, it becomes apparent that no good solution exists. The poorer states will demand equality for their citizens in terms of allocation from the centrally collected taxes, while the richer states will demand fairness in the sharing of the burden and point to the perverse incentive of population growth. The new paradigm would move most revenue collection and expenditure to the points of collection and expenditure. That would mean a significant chunk of the perverse incentives can be sidestepped.

When states, cities and local governments are responsible for their own revenue and expenditure, the conflict over transfer of resources from one region to another becomes moot. This scenario will mean that Karnataka, Tamil Nadu, Telangana and Kerala will not have to worry about contributing to other states' budgets at the expense of their own; they also will have a greater degree of freedom in determining policy that works for their citizens.

What will remain an issue under such a system, though, is the most basic form of that question: What is the obligation of a relatively prosperous state/region if a poor state isn't able to provide basic services such as health, education or security to its people? How will this new paradigm resolve that, if at all it can?

An extreme answer is: If a given region thinks it is too good for the Union, it'll probably try to walk out. But the probability of that is low.

What most states in the Union that want to be in the Union and are wanted by other states in the Union will likely do is converge at a lower bound (a floor) of per capita expense to afford basic services, and an upper bound (a ceiling) of transfers to limit the burden. That would mean a lightly held Union.

Kerala and Tamil Nadu, for example, would be able to tailor their education programmes to optimize output metrics. They would craft their health policies for long-term and geriatric care, given the age of their population and their relative achievements in basic care already. While doing this, and several other things, they will probably set aside some money for transfer to other states in the Union, based on something like the formula mentioned above.

At the same time, states like Madhya Pradesh, Bihar and Uttar Pradesh would focus on basic preventive healthcare practices for infants and mothers. They probably will use transfers from other states to fund such programmes, but they will have to design and manage this largely by themselves. Having a tax base in step with their expense would also be useful in some ways.

The exact way in which such a system would work is impossible to predict. But what it offers is the hope of a fair structure that reflects the will of the people with sufficient guard rails. Perhaps the trajectory would not work as imagined, but it would place high barriers in the way if an illiberal majoritarian lobby wished to drag our multicultural, multi-ethnic society down the abyss.

Democracy isn't about the outcome but structure. The proposed structure aims to be a fairer and more honest representation of the people's will compared to all the existing ones; it seeks the enthusiastic and sustained consent of the governed.

It may be politically infeasible to bring about such radical changes to the existing political structure. But citizens would do well to think about it anyway because the status quo's future repercussions are inevitable and will be more extreme than anything that the proposed system will result in. Given the extreme divergences between its states and indeed, between regions within the states, India needs more local self-governance and locally formulated policies that address specific local needs. Maybe multiple layers of vetoes and mandatory referenda for new legislation is the answer.

Epilogue

All the ways in which societies organize themselves are unfair to one or more groups within those societies. The only necessary lever for managing any form of social organization in the modern era, therefore, is one that allows for constant change and one that also, hopefully, transmits the will of the people effectively.

India, in the way it was structured after Independence, served the purpose of its times: namely, as a strong Union to thwart the possibility of fragmentation and civil war, which was all too common in post-colonial societies of the mid-twentieth century. That strong Union with its scant regard for states' rights has possibly outlived its utility.

India's states, each larger than many countries, are divergent in every imaginable way – in fact in ways that extend beyond the scope of equalization in a strongly centralized federal union. They diverge in terms of their governance outcomes, the health of their citizens, the education they offer and the economic opportunities they provide.

Southern India is a different country in that regard. Not only are its development outcomes vastly better that northern India's, it also happens to be culturally and linguistically distinct from the north. More crucially, in the current structure, southern India faces a real threat of being reduced to a vassal state that has little to no say in how it is governed or taxed.

Any solution that works in the long term will have to invert the pyramid of the existing power structure by diffusing the powers currently concentrated with the Union. The method of that diffusion, though, must be fair and well thought through.

A hasty inversion – one that happens too quickly despite being the right approach – will only precipitate chaos, or violence, or both, especially given the linguistic, ethnic and religious differences between the various regions and peoples of India. There must be an orderly shift of power away from the Union government and towards the states and local governments.

A re-examination of the structure of democracy and the way in which India's Parliament works offers clues as to how the intractable problem could be managed. A move away from the representative model of democracy to a gamified direct democracy with multiple layers of vetoes could be a way out.

The cost of such a move will, of course, be the absence of a strong Union government that projects strength externally at the cost of its constituent parts. It's a cost worth paying if the reward is enlightened liberalism, or a path towards it, with a conservative structure that offers both rectitude in terms of democratic structure and a shot at utilitarian outcomes for the population.

An India that is less about the Union and more about its constituents and constituencies might be an India more capable of managing its diversity, its divergences and contradictions. In such a Union, people everywhere would feel more equal.

Notes

Introduction

1. Prerna Singh, *How Solidarity Works for Welfare: Subnationalism and Social Development in India*, Cambridge University Press, 2015.
2. T.J.S. George, 'Dravidian Stock. Tejasvi Surya vs CN Annadurai', *The New Indian Express*, 16 May 2021.

Part I

2. Education

1. 'School Enrollment, Tertiary (% gross)', World Bank Data, UNESCO Institute for Statistics, data as of June 2022.
2. Lex Borghans, Bart H.H. Golsteyn, James J. Heckman and John Eric Humphries, 'What Grades and Achievement Tests Measure', *Proceedings of the National Academy of Sciences*, 8 November 2016.
3. Ibid.
4. Janet Lorin, 'Why U.S. Colleges are Rethinking Standardized Tests', Bloomberg.com, 14 March 2022.
5. Raynard Kington and Diana Tisnado, 'Increasing Racial and Ethnic Diversity Among Physicians: An Intervention to Address Health Disparities?', *The Right Thing to Do, The Smart Thing to Do: Enhancing Diversity in the Health Professions: Summary of the*

Symposium on Diversity in Health Professions in Honor of Herbert W. Nickens, M.D., National Academies Press, 2001.

3. Economy

1. Sugata Marjit and Sandip Mitra, 'Convergence in Regional Growth Rates: Indian Research Agenda', *Economic and Political Weekly*, Vol. 31, No. 33, 17 August 1996.
2. In economics, 'Dutch disease' is the apparent causal relationship between increase in the economic development of a specific sector (for example, natural resources) and decline in other sectors (like the manufacturing sector or agriculture). The presumed mechanism is that as revenues increase in a growing sector (or in inflows of foreign aid), the given nation's currency becomes stronger (appreciates) against currencies of other nations (manifest in an exchange rate). This results in the nation's other exports becoming more expensive for other countries to buy, and imports becoming cheaper, making those sectors less competitive. While the term is most often used in the case of discovery of natural resources, it can also refer to 'any development that results in a large inflow of foreign currency, including a sharp surge in natural resource prices, foreign assistance, and foreign direct investment', as explained by Christine Ebrahimzadeh in the article 'Dutch Disease: Wealth Managed Unwisely', *Finance & Development*, 24 February 2020.
3. 'Periodic Labour Force Survey, 2018–19', data from Ministry of Statistics and Programme Implementation.
4. V. Bhaskar, 'A Case of Unequal Fiscal Federalism?', *Economic and Political Weekly*, Vol. 56, No. 30, 25 July 2021.

Part II

1. Population Divergence

1. 'Iran', Data Commons 2022, https://datacommons.org/place/country/IRN.
2. 'Vietnam', Data Commons 2022, https://datacommons.org/place/country/VNM.
3. 'Sri Lanka', Data Commons 2022, https://datacommons.org/place/country/LKA.
4. 'Thailand', Data Commons 2022, https://datacommons.org/place/country/THA.

Part III

3. The Athenian Model

1. Mogens Herman Hansen, translated by J.A. Crook, *The Athenian Democracy in the Age of Demosthenes: Structures, Principles and Ideology*, University of Oklahoma Press, 1999.

A Note on the Author

Nilakantan RS trained as an engineer at Clemson University and is the Chief Data Scientist for one of India's largest fintech firms. His primary interest is designing stable decentralized systems – be they political entities or business-related processes. He has written on India's federal structure for publications such as *The Caravan*, Wire.com and *The Hindu*.